written and directed by
Bill Forsyth

Local Hero

David Manderson
and
Alistair Scott

Illustrations by Kev Harper

Association for Scottish Literary Studies 2011

Published by
Association for Scottish Literary Studies
Scottish Literature
7 University Gardens
University of Glasgow
Glasgow G12 8QH
www.asls.org.uk

ASLS is a registered charity no. SC006535

First published 2011

A CIP catalogue for this title
is available from the British Library

ISBN 978-1-906841-04-1

The Association for Scottish Literary Studies
acknowledges the support of Creative Scotland
towards the publication of this book.

CONTENTS

SCOTNOTES

Study guides to major Scottish writers and literary texts

Produced by the Education Committee
of the Association for Scottish Literary Studies

THE ASSOCIATION FOR SCOTTISH LITERARY STUDIES aims to promote the study, teaching and writing of Scottish literature, and to further the study of the languages of Scotland.

To these ends, the ASLS publishes works of Scottish literature; literary criticism and in-depth reviews of Scottish books in *Scottish Literary Review*; short articles, features and news in *ScotLit*; and scholarly studies of language in *Scottish Language*. It also publishes *New Writing Scotland*, an annual anthology of new poetry, drama and short fiction, in Scots, English and Gaelic. ASLS has also prepared a range of teaching materials covering Scottish language and literature for use in schools.

All the above publications are available as a single 'package', in return for an annual subscription. Enquiries should be sent to:

ASLS
Scottish Literature
7 University Gardens
University of Glasgow
Glasgow G12 8QH

Tel/fax +44 (0)141 330 5309
e-mail **office@asls.org.uk**
or visit our website at **www.asls.org.uk**

A poor life this if, full of care,
We have no time to stand and stare.

from *Leisure* by W.H. Davies (lines printed on the
cover of the production script of *Local Hero*)

1. INTRODUCTION

Local Hero, written and directed by Bill Forsyth and produced by David Puttnam, is one of the most important and influential films ever made in Scotland. Released in 1983, it is now considered one of Forsyth's most important films, and he is acknowledged as one of Scotland's greatest directors (Murray, 2011, 1), an artist whose work contributed much towards the making of a Scottish film industry, if such a thing exists. Whether it does or not, his body of work also amounts to a significant strain within British and European film.

But *Local Hero* did more than top the list of Forsyth's work: it also had a huge influence on a whole generation of Scottish actors, writers, directors, producers and other workers within the film industry, demonstrating that a home-grown production could gain international recognition and success. The fact that many people involved were Scottish allowed a new generation of young Scottish filmmakers to believe that they too could make films that would be successful. It promoted a belief among Scottish actors, writers, directors and producers in the possibilities of an indigenous Scottish film industry, and it was a major influence on succeeding films, demonstrating that big budget productions could be made in Scotland using local talent. It is doubtful that without Forsyth's example bigger-budget films which followed would have ever been made. In 2009 BAFTA Scotland (the British Academy of Film & Television Arts) recognised this by awarding Forsyth a Lifetime Achievement Award.

And yet, a decade after its release, *Local Hero* was virtually forgotten. Although recognised as a milestone in Scottish filmmaking, it tended to be considered as part of an interesting but whimsical director's work, or to be patronisingly dismissed by critics as lightweight, a mildly comic story that had made little impact on 'serious' Scottish themes and did not bear comparison with more 'important' movies (Murray, 2011, 2). As more films began to be produced in or about Scotland, *Local Hero's* achievements came to be seen as outdated. In its time the biggest budget film ever made in Scotland, it was overshadowed later by other blockbusters

1

such as *Rob Roy* (Caton-Jones, 1995) and *Braveheart* (Gibson, 1995). It brought to Scotland one of Hollywood's biggest stars, but later films did the same. It employed dozens of Scottish actors and crew, but later films would use many more. In other words, as the public and the film making world grew more blasé about film production in Scotland, the value of *Local Hero* as a film became increasingly neglected. In common with other aspects of Scottish artistic life such as literature or painting, where there is sometimes also a tendency towards 'cultural amnesia' – or a habit of ignoring recent achievements in the rush to move forward to exciting new forms of expression – the debt owed to Forsyth by later filmmakers and screenwriters is considerable, and in many ways remains to be paid.

This survey hopes to redress this balance and to reconsider the true importance and impact of this Scottish film, which showed beyond any doubt how an idiosyncratic, offbeat, funny story about relationships and the ways local communities are treated in the modern world could be a popular hit at home and all over the rest of the world. It will do this by looking at some aspects of the film such as its sources of inspiration, its characters and themes in some detail, including its key concern with protecting and preserving the environment, and also at the way Forsyth, in his script, consistently aims for a kind of bittersweet humour expressed in small moments of realisation, or sudden comic insights into character or situations. This is often done through his dialogue, which seeks constantly to find ways of showing the absurdity of a character's situation. Famous examples of Forsyth's poignant and comic lines are scattered throughout this book.

But in addition, this *Scotnote* seeks to examine the story of *Local Hero*'s production, of what lay behind and beyond the making of the film. It tells the story of the making of the film – of what led to it and what came after it – to show its origins within Scottish film culture and the impact it had on the Scottish film industry and the rest of the world. The aim is to illustrate that what we see on the big screen is only one part of the process, and that what goes into the making of a film, from the casting to the camerawork to the careers of everyone involved, helps shape what we see in the cinema.

ARCHIE: Are you sure there are two l's in dollar, Gideon?
GIDEON: Yes ... And are there two g's in bugger off?

2. BILL FORSYTH: THE APPRENTICESHIP OF A WRITER/DIRECTOR

Bill Forsyth served a long apprenticeship in the film industry, during which he worked his way slowly up the ranks of the business, from making the tea for a tiny Glasgow documentary film production company to directing films for a major Hollywood studio. Many of his experiences during this apprenticeship would influence his approach when writing and directing *Local Hero*.

Forsyth was born in Glasgow in 1946, the son of a plumber, and grew up in the Whiteinch district of the city near the River Clyde. He left school with no clear career aspirations until he spotted an advert in the local paper: 'Lad required for film production business – Maryhill' (Donlon, 2008). He applied for the job and in February 1964, aged seventeen, he started work earning £3 per week with the pioneer film producer Stanley Russell at Thames & Clyde Films.

Like a number of other small Scottish companies Thames & Clyde produced documentaries and educational shorts which were called 'sponsored films', although today they would probably be called 'corporates'. This was the era of a government agency, 'Films of Scotland', which commissioned short documentaries about various aspects of contemporary life in Scotland (Sherington). Subjects for Films of Scotland documentaries included the traditional heavy industries like shipbuilding; the construction of new towns like East Kilbride and Cumbernauld; and the whisky, tourism and industries in the Highlands and Islands. First with Thames & Clyde, and later with International Film Associates Scotland and other small production companies, Forsyth gained experience in all aspects of documentary film production, working as a camera assistant on location and as an assistant and later editor in the cutting rooms. He has described these short films as 'glorified magic lantern shows, pictures with words' (Robertson, 2009) which tried to capture the speed and energy of the changes taking place in the Scotland of the 1960s. They did this by means of striking and insistent images which showed

4

seemingly everyday things – smoke belching from factory chimneys, or steel running white-hot from furnaces – in arresting visual ways. (In fact, according to Forsyth himself, Stanley Russell encouraged his young assistant to see filming as like 'looking at puddles': noticing commonplace yet unique things and stringing them together in an order.) (Robertson, 2009) They were filmic moments crucial to each subject which the camera deliberately lingered on.

By the end of the decade Forsyth was eager to move on to bigger and better films and to establish himself as a director. He had been experimenting as a filmmaker with personal projects. His short film, *Waterloo*, was screened at the 1970 Edinburgh Film Festival where it was received indifferently (most of the audience walked out) (Donlon, 2008). In the same year, the National Film School was established at Beaconsfield Studios just outside London, funded by the government to train a new generation of filmmakers. The director of the NFS was Colin Young, a Scot who had been teaching at the film school at the University of California in Los Angeles. In his trips to publicise the new course at the NFS, Young had come to Scotland and met those working in the close-knit Scottish film industry. Forsyth saw this as an opportunity and applied for the course. In 1971 he joined the first intake of students. But his roots were firmly in Scotland and he spent more time commuting to and from Glasgow than making projects at Beaconsfield. Although he formed important lasting friendships with Colin Young and other students such as the future feature film director, Mike Radford, after just one year he dropped out.

Back in Scotland, he set up a new documentary production company in partnership with fellow Glasgow-based filmmaker, Charlie Gormley. Their production company, Tree Films, ran from 1972–79. Together Gormley and Forsyth produced the usual portfolio of documentaries and sponsored films, including projects about the infant North Sea oil industry, but they were also determined to put together more ambitious projects. Throughout the 1970s these two filmmakers, like many in the Scottish film community, dreamed of making movies. In 1977 this group of people came together at a conference in Glasgow entitled *Cinema in a Small Country*, which looked at the experience of making feature films in other European countries. But despite all the debate it seemed impossible to pursue this ambition in Scotland. In 1976 Tree Films travelled to Ecuador to produce a documentary film that followed an international expedition to the prehistoric cave system made famous by the theories of Erich von Daniken. Three years later, the film was completed as *The Legend of Los Tayos* and sold to television. It was Forsyth and Gormley's last joint project. After seven years together their business folded and they parted company to develop their own careers.

Released from the pressure of running a company, Forsyth devoted himself to writing the feature film script which would become *Gregory's Girl*, a contemporary story about teenagers growing up in Cumbernauld, then still a very new Scottish 'New Town'. It was a setting he knew well from his work on many sponsored documentaries. *Gregory's Girl* was a coming-of-age story that also contained romance, football and comedy, a combination that Forsyth felt sure would be successful; however, he was unable to interest any producers in the project. As part of his research into potential actors he spent time visiting the regular sessions of the Glasgow Youth Theatre and began work on a new script designed to showcase the talents of the young amateur actors he met there. He was determined to make this drama as a low budget film using the sixteen-millimetre equipment normally used on documentaries.[1] He gathered together a production crew and team of technicians from the small Scottish film industry community, who all agreed to defer their salaries as an investment. Filmed over the 1979 Easter holiday, *That Sinking Feeling*, a comedy about four unemployed teenage boys who plan to steal stainless steel sinks from a local factory in an attempt to escape the monotony of their everyday lives, was made on a shoestring cash budget of under £6000. The film was launched at the 1979 Edinburgh Film Festival and, with its wry, deadpan humour and engaging natural performances, soon began to build an enthusiastic and appreciative audience. Despite its miniscule budget it felt like a real movie.

Forsyth had lit the touch paper for the explosive beginning of a film industry in Scotland.

His next step was to raise the budget for a more substantial, properly funded production. Also in 1979, an international feature film production came to Scotland, shot entirely on location in Glasgow. *Death Watch*, by French director Bernard Tavernier, was a science fiction story with a cast which included American actors Harvey Keitel, Harry Dean Stanton and Romy Schneider. A number of local production crew and technicians, including cameraman Michael Coulter and location manager Iain Smith, worked on the film, gaining further experience of big-budget filmmaking and demonstrating to film professionals and the world at large that Scottish technicians did have the skills required to make commercial feature films.

As *That Sinking Feeling* was screened around the country and gradually gained distribution, Forsyth returned to the task of regaining interest in the script of *Gregory's Girl*. He now had a track record in the film industry, demonstrating his ability both to tell a story and to direct young actors. On the strength of this, producers Clive Parsons and Davina Belling of Film & General Productions agreed to develop the project. With Forsyth, they raised a budget of £200,000, half from the National Film Finance Corporation and half from Scottish Television. It was still a relatively modest sum but it was enough to go into production in the spring of 1980.

As he worked on casting the actors for *Gregory's Girl*, Forsyth returned to the youngsters who had worked on *That Sinking Feeling* along with other actors from professional Scottish theatre companies. The production team also included crew members who had worked on the earlier film and others who had gained experience on *Death Watch*. *Gregory's Girl* is a comedy, full of unexpected and sometimes unexplained incidents, about life at secondary school, showing how an awkward teenager, Gregory (played by John Gordon Sinclair – for further details of the actors involved in the making of *Local Hero* see Section 9), discovers love against the backdrop of the tribulations of a struggling school football team. *Gregory's Girl* was premiered at the 1980

London Film Festival and released in 1981 to a very positive
critical reaction. Soon it had become a hit with British audiences. Forsyth had completed his apprenticeship. His films
had broken through into mainstream cinema, and his work
was starting to receive recognition. He was ready for an even
bigger project.

In 1982 he received the BAFTA Award for Best Original
Screenplay for *Gregory's Girl*. On the same night *Chariots
of Fire* producer, David Puttnam, was presented with the
BAFTA for Best Film by American movie star Burt Lancaster.
It was a night which would be an important turning point in
the making of *Local Hero*.

3. *LOCAL HERO*:
THE MAKING OF A FILM

How the project started

From the outset, *Local Hero* was a collaboration between Forsyth and the producer David Puttnam. Puttnam had established himself as a leading British film producer after a career in commercials. His early films included *The Duellists* and *Midnight Express*. He had been introduced to Bill Forsyth by the National Film School Director, Colin Young, in 1979, when *That Sinking Feeling* was gathering favourable reviews. Forsyth had tried earlier to get Puttnam to take on the role of producer for *Gregory's Girl*, but Puttnam had turned it down, having already made a coming-of-age story with *That'll Be the Day* (Whatham, 1973).

At the same time, Puttnam was working with the director, Hugh Hudson, and the writer, Colin Welland, on the development of a film about the British athletes at the 1922 Paris Olympic Games. One of the central characters was Scotsman Eric Liddell. When *Chariots of Fire* went into production in 1980, a local Scottish production crew, including location manager Iain Smith, was hired to film the scenes set on location in Scotland. It was more proof to the film industry of the way Scottish crews could support major films. The film was launched at the 1981 Cannes Film Festival and proved to be an international hit, going on to win the Academy Award for Best Film the following year.

Puttnam had already had the germ of an idea for a new film which would be about preserving the environment, and which he thought would be right for a writer/director like Forsyth. He sent Forsyth an envelope of press cuttings about the impact of the North Sea oil industry on remote communities in the north of Scotland. Puttnam had long admired the work of film producer Michael Balcon, who had run the Ealing Studios in the 1950s. When Forsyth was in London putting the finishing touches to *Gregory's Girl*, Puttnam invited him to a screening room, where together they watched an Ealing comedy, produced by Balcon and directed by Alexander Mackendrick. *Whisky Galore!* is an adaptation

9

of Compton Mackenzie's novel, based on a true story, about how the population of a Hebridean island manages to dupe the authorities and salvage the contents of a freighter after it is wrecked carrying a cargo of thousands of cases of Scotch whisky. Puttnam wanted to make a modern-day film with the same ingredients, where wily Scots from the communities of the Highlands and Islands outwit the representatives of capitalism and authority. The contemporary twist was that this would be a story about the oil industry.

Over the next few months Forsyth worked on the script, encouraged by the growing commercial success of *Gregory's Girl*. He also gathered further experience as a writer/director by working on a BBC television adaptation of a short story by Orkney writer George Mackay Brown, entitled *Andrina* (Forsyth, 1981). The ideas for *Local Hero* were gradually taking shape, with inspirations that moved the original premise forward in unexpected ways. Early in the process, Forsyth came up with the character of the American oil tycoon, Felix Happer, owner of Knox Oil, and almost immediately thought of the veteran movie star Burt Lancaster in the role. He had delivered the completed script to Puttnam's company Enigma Films, and the process of putting together finance from different investors was already under way, when, on the night of the BAFTA Awards in early 1982, Puttnam, Forsyth and Lancaster found themselves all in the same room together. On the same evening, and after both *Chariots of Fire* and *Gregory's Girl* had picked up awards, Puttnam was approached by James Lee from financiers, Goldcrest Productions. They had been one of the investors in *Chariots* and had already agreed to put up part of the money for *Local Hero*. Buoyed by the success of the evening, Lee agreed to find the outstanding shortfall, and the production was given the final green light to move into production. *Local Hero* had found its budget and its star in the same evening.

The script
It is important to consider Forsyth as both a director *and* a writer. Writing and directing a feature film is relatively

unusual. Usually, a producer develops a script with a writer over a period of time and engages a director when the script is in its later stages. The director uses the script as a blueprint, imposing his own vision and changing the original as he wishes. But in *Local Hero*'s case, the script was the director's vision, which gave it an unusual importance in the making of the film.

Local Hero is a fable about what happens when an international oil company sets out to exploit the beach and coastline around a beautiful remote village. As with Forsyth's earlier films, the story consists of sequences of interconnected, often slightly mysterious, and sometimes downright magical incidents. The simplicity of the bare facts of the narrative, which are outlined below, fails to capture either the real story or the humour. Many characters appear only in short cameo roles, and many scenes seem to have no function beyond being comic, yet they make a real impact on the overall atmosphere. A sense of wonder seems to be at the heart of the film's appeal, often encapsulated in the striking lines of dialogue, but the effect is subtle, never exaggerated or forceful. You can never be quite sure of where you are in a Forsyth film, and in order to enjoy it, you really do have to watch and listen carefully.

To achieve his ends, Forsyth the screenwriter uses devices that upset audience expectations, notably **reversal** and **ambiguity**. Reversal is where traditional roles are overturned to comic effect. In *Gregory's Girl*, for example, the adults seem childlike while the children seem cynical and worldly wise. In *Local Hero*, the wealthy Americans seem troubled and lost, in search of a home, while the native Scots are only too happy to sell up and move on. American society with its towers of glass and steel seems claustrophobic and fixed, while an apparently remote Highland village welcomes outsiders: an African minister, a Russian trawler man, a mermaid, a Texan oilman. Ambiguity is where more than one interpretation can be made of a moment or an event and no definite 'answer' is supplied: the different meanings are deliberately left open. The smile Stella gives the helicopter as Mac flies off, the telephone ringing in the kiosk at the film's end, the moment where Marina smiles over her shoulder at Oldsen – these are all ambiguous interactions or happenings, where we are allowed to make our own interpretation.

The film opens in Houston, Texas. An executive, Macintyre (Peter Reigert) is driving to work along the freeway. An announcement on K.N.O.X. Radio indicates that 'Hurricane Eleanor' has been successfully driven back, 'maybe to avoid all that traffic' (see Section 8). Meanwhile at the offices of Knox Oil & Gas a group of businessmen at a conference are watching a documentary film about North Sea oil (just the type of sponsored film Forsyth knew well). The boss, Felix Happer (Burt Lancaster), slumbers through the meeting as his executives talk about their '... acquisition of Scotland ...', and we see a map of Ferness Bay with a price tag of $60 million.

Happer has a passion for astronomy and watching the sky at night. For an unexplained reason he also employs a therapist, Moritz (played by Norman Chancer), to insult him.

> HAPPER: Comets are important.
> MORITZ: Mr Happer's got his comet. Hooray! What an empty, hollow, wasteful activity. You're chasing comets around the sky. Is your life around you so complete? What about a wife, children, a family? Are these human goals too simple for you?

Happer summons Macintyre because he thinks (wrongly) he has Scottish family connections and tells him that he is sending him to Scotland, 'the old country', from where the founder of the Knox company originally emigrated. Most importantly, Mac is ordered to keep an eye on the night sky: '... find the big dipper. The Northern sky's a beautiful thing.'

As he packs for the trip we get a glimpse of Mac's life. He has a fast car and a fancy apartment but no friends and no one to answer his phone calls. Mac arrives in Scotland and is met by the local company representative, Oldsen (Peter Capaldi), who clumsily hides his 'Knox Oil Welcomes' sign and seems unable to keep the project secret. The two men visit a laboratory to see a model of a proposed refinery which will be built on the beach beside the village of Ferness. At the laboratory, while Mac talks to the scientists Geddes (Rikki Fulton) and Norman Watt (Alex Norton), Oldsen meets Marina (Jenny Seagrove) who dives into the experimental tank which we see is a model of the village.

> WATT: She's got a magnificent pair of lungs!

The scientists are enthusiastic about their work and have no concern at all for the effect their plans will have on it. It's 'a bay in a million', one of them proclaims. It is now Mac's job to make the formal contracts to secure the agreement of local villagers in Ferness.

Mac and Oldsen travel by car to the village through the beautiful Scottish Highland landscape but seem to lose their way. Mist comes down and there is a thump as they hit something. It is a rabbit in the middle of the road which they decide to rescue, feed and take with them.

> OLDSEN: Should we put it out of its misery?
> MAC: What do you mean?
> OLDSEN: Kill it. Hit it with something hard.
> MAC: You already did that with a two-ton automobile.

Still lost in the mist, they fall asleep in the car. Mac's watch alarm goes off reminding him that it is conference time in Houston. As the mist rises they see the coast and the beautiful bay looking across to the Scottish islands, but the calm is suddenly broken as a jet fighter plane breaking the sound barrier flies low across the hillside.

They arrive in the village of Ferness in the morning. After being forced to stop by a sleeping dog they arrive at the town's small hotel owned and run by Gordon Urquhart (Denis Lawson) and his wife Stella (Jennifer Black). Gordon and Stella, who seem to have other things on their minds, look out from the bedroom window as Mac informs them that they want to check in, and: 'We have an injured rabbit also ...'. Gordon is a man of many jobs: hotelier, accountant

and advisor on business affairs. After breakfast Mac explains
to Gordon that he represents Knox Oil and wants to buy the
village. It is clear that Gordon and all the rest of the community already know that the American company is interested in
building some sort of oil facility and they are all keen to make
as much money as possible from the new development.

There are a number of familiar local characters who seem
ever present, including local teenage biker Ricky (John
Gordon Sinclair), who is a constant threat to pedestrians in
the tiny, isolated village. The local people seem more than
mildly eccentric, their characters, even those who appear only
momentarily on the screen (the woman played by veteran
Scottish actress Ida Shuster, who is present at the ceilidh,
is one example), explored in one small scene after another:
revealing and funny moments, tiny but important, played
with Forsyth's characteristic understatement.

> POSTMISTRESS: Good afternoon.
> MAC: Hello. I'd like some toothpaste. Something with
> fluoride or ammonia. And some shampoo.
> POSTMISTRESS: Dry, normal or greasy?
> MAC: Normal ... Extra normal.
>   *POSTMISTRESS hands over shampoo.*
> POSTMISTRESS: That's normal. That'll do your dandruff
> as well.

After dinner Gordon shows Mac the village and the beach.
It is stunningly beautiful, an idealised vision of Scotland.
Whilst Mac walks along the sand his watch alarm buzzes:
Houston time. Back at the jetty he borrows some change to
phone his office from the local telephone box. He tells his
colleague in Houston 'It feels like I've been here forever'. As
Mac stretches out in his bedroom listening to Gordon and
Stella making love upstairs Trudy the rabbit twitches her
whiskers sitting in the armchair. Back in Houston, Happer
is having a loud argument with his therapist, Moritz.

The next day as Mac walks along the beach again, he spots
one of the local characters, Ben (Fulton MacKay), who lives in
a ramshackle hut by the shore and collects the flotsam which

washes in on the tide. Meanwhile there is a meeting in the church: the whole village, led by Gordon Urquhart, is trying to work out how to make as much money as possible from the oil company. To distract Mac's attention the minister, a black African, the Rev. Murdo McPherson (Christopher Asante), is dispatched to talk to him. The men stand watching the planes practising their low-flying manoeuvres over the bay, and bombing the hillsides. 'As long as they're bombing the beach they can't be bombing anywhere else', the minister explains. As Mac watches he fails to see the villagers streaming from the church behind him.

> MAC: We're on kind of a mission.
> REV McPHERSON: Me too.

At dinner Gordon serves up 'casserole de lapin' and as he finishes the delicious meal Mac gradually realises he has just eaten the rabbit. The next day as Gordon and Stella find yet another time and place to make love, Mac and Oldsen return to the beach. Mac is getting to know the locals. Oldsen sees Marina, the girl from the laboratory, diving in the bay. She explains how she has found baby coral growing and that 'This is my bay ... I'm plotting everything.' Meanwhile, it is clear that Mac is becoming more and more entranced by the village. He does not bother to try to negotiate with Gordon any more; he is more interested in trying a forty two year old malt. Meanwhile the villagers are planning their trust funds.

Mac and Gordon visit Ben outside his shack and ask how much he thinks the bay was worth. Ben laughs at the question. As they leave there is a meteor shower in the night sky. They watch it transfixed. A little later, back in the hotel, we see Oldsen in the bathtub holding his breath under water, as if he is trying to live underwater. The following morning, as Mac and Oldsen leave the hotel, the phone in the telephone box is ringing. A villager, Iain (Jimmy Yuill), who always accompanies Mac to the telephone box, shouts for Mac: 'It's a Mr Houston'. Happer is ringing from his planetarium at Knox Oil. From the phone kiosk Mac relates the news of last

night's meteor shower and possible news of potential comet
activity in the constellation of Leo. Later, we see Happer cook
a lonely omelette and lose his temper with the mad therapist
Moritz.

The next day once again Mac and Oldsen are exploring
different parts of the beach. Mac is now barefoot, pottering
in a rockpool. Marina appears next to Oldsen and together
they watch the seals. 'Sailors used to believe they were
mermaids', she tells him. Back in the village shop a Russian
trawlerman calls in on the CB radio. He is a regular visitor
planning to arrive in time for the forthcoming ceilidh. Mrs
Wyatt (Karen Black) passes on the news: 'Roddy – tell
Gordon Urquhart the Russians are coming'. When Victor
(Christopher Rozycki) does arrive by boat in the harbour,
clutching bottles of vodka, Gordon explains, 'We've been
invaded by America'.

Mac is wandering alone on the beach collecting shells.
He leaves his watch submerged under water, its alarm now
muted. On another part of the shore Oldsen is teaching
Marina words from various foreign languages. They get
closer and start to kiss: Oldsen kisses down Marina's leg to
her foot. As communist fisherman Victor checks his stock
market investments in the hotel bar, the village prepares
for the ceilidh. At the dance we hear the band, the Ace
Tones, play, and watch various different characters. The
whole village is there including Ben, who scavenges cakes
and sandwiches from the spread on the table. Mac is slowly
getting tipsy. Various villagers talk about the possible
windfall that they expect from the oil company and Victor
toasts their good fortune.

> VICTOR: It's their place, Mac. They have a right to make
> what they can of it. You can't eat scenery!

The only person who doesn't welcome the development is
Marina, to whom Oldsen reveals the news of the oil refinery.
But she takes the news calmly, as if she already knows what
the future holds: 'No I don't see that happening here. I don't
see that at all'.

In the night sky above the village hall the Northern Lights are suddenly visible. Mac comes out to the telephone box to phone Happer on his private number: 'I'm watching the sky, sir – It's doing some amazing things. It's got everything. Reds, greens ... I wish you could see it ... Wow, it's blue! ... It's the 'rora borealis. It's beautiful.' As Happer takes the call back in the Houston office the therapist is outside the window with a banner which reads: 'Happer is a motherfu—'. Happer leaves the office giving his secretary instructions to call the police: 'There's a maniac outside the building. You'd better call the police department. Shoot him off. Shoot to kill.' Meanwhile at the ceilidh the villagers muse over their newfound wealth.

> PETER: Well Edward, I wonder what the poor people are doing tonight.
> EDWARD: Aye but Peter – I thought all this money would make me feel – well – different ...
> PETER: What do you mean?
> EDWARD: Well all it's done is make me feel depressed. I don't feel any different ...
> PETER: Well Edward, you'll just need to buck up. You need to accept the fact that you're stinking rich. Nobody ever said it was going to be easy to be a millionaire, Edward.

At the end of the evening, now more drunk than tipsy, Mac has a proposition for Gordon. He wants to swap lives with him: 'Take the Porsche, the house, the job ... I want you to have it all. I'll make a good Gordon, Gordon.' But he wants Gordon to give him Stella in exchange.

The next day they discover that there is a problem. The beach belongs to Ben, having been given to his family four hundred years ago. Mac, Gordon and Victor go to the shack to try to persuade Ben to sell and for the first time Mac discovers that Ben's surname is Knox, as in Knox Oil. When offered money for the beach Ben explains: 'I'm still working the place myself'. Mac tries to do a deal by offering any beach he wants – 'five or six miles of Hawaii?' But Ben replies: 'I only need the one ... I'm not sure that there's a living in those

other beaches.' As a compromise Ben offers him the beach
for a pound for every grain of sand in a handful of sand. But
Mac is confused and cannot do business like this. He has
been tricked by the supposedly much less worldly local man,
a foreshadowing of what will come later when Ben meets
Happer. After eating a good dinner back at the hotel Mac
and Gordon walk Ben back to the beach, feeling a sense of
menace from the other villagers. And they have reason to
fear for the elderly man: the whole population of the village
wants to 'have a word' with Ben, and streams down to the
beach in a dark mirroring of the comic way they streamed
from the church earlier. But suddenly everyone is distracted
by an unnaturally bright light in the sky (see Section 4). It is
the searchlight from a helicopter.

Happer lands on the beach as the crowd of villagers starts
to disperse. He mistakes this for a special reception committee and also mistakes Oldsen for Macintyre, but he is pleased
with the stars: 'Good sky, well done ... Get me a telescope.'
The next day, once Happer realises the situation, he and Ben
get to know each other. After their meeting Happer has been
persuaded that the village will be much more suitable for a
research institute, probably named after himself: 'Sea and sky.
I like that – the Happer Institute.' The beach will be saved. Mac
is sent off in the helicopter back to Houston and sees Stella
hanging out her underwear on the washing line as he flies
over the village, past the telephone box, along the beach and
up a loch into the highland glens, where the mist still hangs.
On the beach Marina, in her wet suit dives into the waves
and Oldsen, fully dressed, follows, splashing his way into the
water. We catch a glimpse of what might be a mermaid's tail.
Back in Houston, Mac arrives back at his lonely apartment
and look out over the flashing lights of the city at night. He
pulls shells from his trouser pockets and surveys his empty
apartment and the city. In Ferness we hear the phone ringing
in the telephone box on the jetty. No one answers.

Getting the movie made
The production had gained green-light status on the night of
the BAFTA Awards in early 1982 and with funding agreed

the team was able to move into full pre-production with the shoot planned for the late spring and early summer. This would mean speedily confirming cast and crew, finding locations that would capture the places envisaged in the script, and planning a schedule.

Casting is fundamental to the success of feature films. Producers will often identify 'above the line' talent, meaning well-known actors who will generate potential investment (in many cases, no matter what the project is), because these stars ensure that the audience will be attracted to the film. From the outset Forsyth had seen veteran Hollywood star Burt Lancaster in the role of American oil tycoon Felix Happer, but, although the film did gain a major star's services, the casting of *Local Hero* was unusual. Happer is not the film's protagonist but an eccentric figure who sets the story in motion, looms in the background (with a sub-plot involving a series of comic encounters with his therapist) and appears in the closing scenes to determine the resolution. The role appealed to Lancaster precisely because it was different and comic – a new challenge after a career of many movies as a leading actor.

The main story of the film follows other characters, Mac and Oldsen, the two young company representatives of Knox Oil who come to Ferness to negotiate the acquisition of the village. Mac is the main protagonist, an ideal part for a young American at the beginning of his career, a role demanding an actor able to change from a pushy young professional to someone who learns that his normal life is lonely and empty, and that the lifestyle and values of a remote community are more attractive than a fast Porsche and a plush executive apartment.

Rather than work with big name talent, Forsyth spotted Peter Reigert, who had worked on *Animal House*. Reigert seemed to bring the right mix of naivety and humour to the role of the incomer who gradually falls under the spell of the village. Many other newcomers and relatively inexperienced actors gained a first chance to shine on the big screen in the film. For Danny Oldsen, Knox Oil's Scottish rep, Forsyth cast the unknown Peter Capaldi, who had just graduated from art school with no professional experience. Capaldi's performance brought Oldsen's character to life with an awkward, gangly physicality and charm. Forsyth had also written a full range of over twenty characters to populate the fictional village of Ferness. Casting these parts involved bringing together new and experienced Scottish talents. These included the established television actor Fulton MacKay (well-known from his role as a prison officer in the BBC sitcom *Porridge*) as Ben the beachcomber, and emerging film actor Dennis Lawson, fresh from a small role in *Star Wars*, as Gordon. For Stella and Marina, the idealised siren spirits of female allure (see Section 7), Forsyth cast the young actresses Jennifer Black and Jenny Seagrove, both in their first major film roles, one from Scottish theatre and the other almost straight from drama college. The rest of the villagers were played by an ensemble of Scottish actors, including veterans such as Willie Joss and Charlie Kearney, well-established professionals such as Kenny Ireland as Skipper and Dave Anderson (who plays Gregory's dad in *Gregory's Girl*) as Fraser, and youngsters such as Caroline Guthrie, Jonathan Watson and John Gordon Sinclair. There were also cameo scenes for Christopher Asante, as the black African minister, the Rev. Murdo Macpherson, Chris Rozycki as Victor, the skipper of a Russian trawler boat, and Rikki Fulton and Alex Norton as Geddes and Watt, the white-coated scientists in charge of their sophisticated marine laboratory. For many of the actors in this large cast, even those with relatively small roles, the film would provide an important step in gaining wider recognition on the screen.

As decisions were finalised on the cast, Forsyth and Puttnam also settled on Mark Knopfler, the front man of the band Dire Straits, as the composer for the film (see Section 5). His Celtic-inspired guitar riffs would create a haunting underscore. Mark and other members of the band agreed to come up to the location and join local musicians to form the ceilidh band the Ace Tones. In this way the score could be subtly interwoven into scenes and action shown in the film.

Getting a film production to run smoothly is also about casting the right crew behind the camera. The production team for *Local Hero* brought together people with experience on previous Puttnam productions with local Scottish technicians who had worked with Forsyth on earlier projects. In this way the film was instrumental in establishing the careers of a number of Scots who would go on to work in the movie industry in both Britain and the USA. In the production department Iain Smith, as Associate Producer, had already worked with both producer and director. As stated earlier, he had been Location Manager for Puttnam on *Chariots of Fire* in 1981, and he had also often worked with Forsyth on the documentaries of the 1970s. (Smith would go on to become a respected producer on large scale movies filmed all over the world – see Section 9.) In the technical departments Chris Menges, an experienced Lighting Cameraman, was brought up from London to lead a team of local technicians led by camera operator Michael Coulter, who had shot *Gregory's Girl*. After *Local Hero* Coulter moved on to become a Director of Photography in his own right and would work in Britain and Hollywood, being nominated for the Academy Award for Best Photography for *Sense and Sensibility*.

At the same time as casting, the other main challenge during the pre-production period was to find real locations to film the vision of Scotland set out in the script. Production Designer Roger Murray-Leach scoured the coast of Scotland to find a fishing village with a suitably expansive and beautiful beach. But the more he searched, the more conscious he became that Ferness was a fantasy of a Scotland which did not really exist. Eventually the team decided to create the setting by using two locations on opposite sides of the country. For the beach, filming took place on the west coast at Camusdarroch Beach, south of Mallaig, looking across to the Cuillin Mountains on the Isle of Skye. For the village, they used the tiny hamlet of Pennan in Banffshire on the north east coast, where there really is a row of white-painted fishermen's houses around a small harbour. The team were aware that this had echoes of a previous movie depiction of

Scotland. According to legend, when Hollywood producer
Arthur Freed and director Vincent Minnelli were looking
for locations to film *Brigadoon* (1948) they came to hunt for
locations in Scotland but famously declared that they could
not find anywhere that looked Scottish enough, so they
returned to Los Angeles and built their fantasy vision in the
studio.[2]

Forsyth has stated that, documentary maker as he was,
he did not realise that one realistic-looking fictional place
could be made out of two locations until the technical people
working with him on the film showed him how it could be
done. He was astonished to learn that it was possible to
stitch together his vision of the village and the beach by
filming in two different places. But it duly was, with the
shots in the west coast being filmed first before everyone in
the production packed up and headed over to the east coast.
The move, he has said in an interview (Forsyth, 2008), was
like a travelling circus, everyone laden with gear as they
headed across country, each vehicle following the other
in a caravan. But it is a tribute not just to the skill of the
crew, but to the strength and conviction of Forsyth's original
vision, that the fictional village of Ferness, the town and the
beach together, rings true, to the extent that visitors today
to the real village of Pennan are often disappointed that no
beach exists. In fact, when we watch *Local Hero* we take
from it above all a haunting sense of place. If place is important to a drama, and helps convince us that the events we
are watching matter and are in some way meaningful, then
Forsyth and his team overcame the challenge of the location
with superb skill.

Filming began on in April 1982 with a schedule that
started in Houston, Texas. Lancaster had committed to
the film and was involved from day one of the shoot, but
he was only prepared (and available) to give a limited
number of days to the project, and so it was crucial that
the production arrange his scenes as effectively as possible.
This meant that they needed to guarantee that they would
use him at all times, whatever the weather, on the days
he came to Scotland. In order to make this possible they

had to have 'weather cover', so that they could film interior as well as exterior scenes. The script was tailored so that Happer would never appear in the village, only on the beach, meaning that Lancaster would only be involved in the filming on the west coast. The set for Happer's private office at Knox Oil headquarters in Houston was built in a distillery warehouse in Fort William, near the beach, so that whatever the weather there would be no hold-ups when filming with him. Lancaster travelled to Scotland in early May and his scenes were amongst the first completed at the Camusdarroch Beach. In fact the late spring weather was perfect and meant that snow still lay on the tops of the mountains of Skye, visible in the background as Happer strides along the beach chatting with Ben as they devise a plan for a new research institute. After Lancaster's scenes had been completed the unit moved across to the village of Pennan on the east coast and filming continued.

The schedule was structured so that many of the ensemble of village characters were on call throughout many of the shooting days, giving the production team the flexibility needed to take advantage of good weather for the major set piece scenes, such as when the whole village creeps from the church when Mac is distracted by the minister, and when everyone comes out to the harbour to greet Victor, the Russian trawler skipper. The unit established an editing room in one of the local hotels so that film editor Mike Bradsell was able to put together a first rough cut as filming was proceeding. There were some issues about properly checking material for projection on a big screen because the locations were so far from the film processing laboratory.[3] The last scene to be completed was shot later in the summer when the marine laboratory and the model of Ferness and the beach were built in a studio outside London.

There was great excitement throughout the period of shooting. The reputations of both Puttnam and Forsyth were riding high. With both having recently won awards, and a big American star in Scotland, there was a real sense of anticipation. This led to wide press interest and a constant stream of documentary television crews record-

ing the film's progress.[4] The buzz of publicity benefited the
production company, as soon after filming began Puttnam
secured a deal with Warner Brothers for the North American
distribution rights, ensuring that the feature would gain a
successful release.

4. *LOCAL HERO*:
STYLE AND INFLUENCES

Local Hero was the first big movie to be written and directed by Bill Forsyth, but the tone of the film and his unique director's voice goes back to the influences throughout his apprenticeship starting in 1964. He had learned a great deal from his long training with documentary, especially the importance of the offbeat, lingering moment. His sense of absurdity, the lightness and yet seriousness of his humour, and his ability to incorporate scenes where little insights reveal the simple foibles of the main characters, led to critics describing his style as whimsical and quirky, and linking it to earlier film makers such as Frank Capra. It was a judgement that verged on misunderstanding the film's originality and underestimating its real achievement, and it did not always assist the film in later years.

Forsyth insisted that every copy of the production script had a short quotation from a Welsh poet on the cover:

> A poor life this if, full of care,
> We have no time to stand and stare.

The lines are from *Leisure* by W. H. Davies:

> What is this life if, full of care,
> We have no time to stand and stare?—
>
> No time to stand beneath the boughs,
> And stare as long as sheep and cows:
>
> No time to see, when woods we pass,
> Where squirrels hide their nuts in grass:
>
> No time to see, in broad daylight,
> Streams full of stars, like skies at night.

The poem helps us understand Forsyth's voice, a filmmaker who finds magic and irony in the events of everyday life. It stresses the importance of just looking, of understanding what we are experiencing through simply being aware of what is around us, and seeing ordinary things, especially natural ones, in a completely new way.

But the film had many influences. There was a conscious reference to sponsored films. As Mac arrives for his early morning meeting at Knox Oil the audience is drawn into a sponsored documentary about Scotland and oil exploration which would have been familiar to Forsyth (and all the Scots working on the crew). The later scene in the marine laboratory with the scientists Geddes and Watt is also reminiscent of many documentaries which featured visions of the hi-tech future.

The film's plot also acknowledges earlier Scottish films: the incoming American frustrated by the local community in the British Ealing comedy *The Maggie;* the incoming American falling under the spell of a village community in *Brigadoon;* the incomer leaving the city and discovering her true desires in *I Know Where I'm Going* (Powell & Pressburger, 1948); the ceilidh as a key event which brings together the community and encourages the protagonists to go native in all these films. The ceilidh in Scottish films is inevitably a pivotal scene, a night of dance, drink and delirium where characters change, fall in love or experience the mysterious magic of the Highlands in some other way, and *Local Hero* is no exception – indeed, it deliberately plays on this tradition. The ceilidh is a crucial central scene in the film. Oldsen is pursued by the punk girl (Caroline Guthrie) but makes his escape. Victor the Russian communist is shown to be in a relationship with Mrs Wyatt the Postmistress, perhaps explaining why his wife, the Russian woman who brought him to the harbour in a dinghy, was furious as she dropped him off. He is a Russian fisherman, who also plays the stock market with Gordon Urquhart's assistance, and clambers up on stage to sing an emotional version of *Lone Star Man*, a Texan Country & Western song that illustrates Mac's loneliness. Characters shed their inhibitions and reveal their real selves. The veteran actress Ida Shuster, who has no lines in the film, listens entranced as the Ace Tones play a moody acoustic version of the film's theme music, and in particular the section taken from the traditional air *Chi mi na morbheanna* (*The Mist-Covered Mountains*), one of the most beautiful Gaelic songs (see Section 5).

Other themes in these earlier films are also echoed in *Local Hero*. The way the community tries to outsmart authority and the big shot from overseas is a modern version of the stories of the two films, *Whisky Galore!* and *The Maggie*, which were both directed by Scot Sandy Mackendrick. The canniness of the wily and resourceful locals under their apparent lack of sophistication is constantly stressed in affectionate and funny moments.

> ARCHIE: Four generations have worked that farm. Digging and draining and planting. Years and years and it comes to this.
> SANDY: Aye, strange times, Archie. What was it Gordon Urquhart offered you?
> ARCHIE: One and a half million in cash plus two percent of the relocation fund and a share in the oil field revenue.
> SANDY: Aye, strange times, strange times.
> *They dance*

The sense of ancient magic is also present in many of these films, especially *I Know Where I'm Going* and *Brigadoon*. There are specific echoes of both these texts in incidents in *Local Hero*. The scene where the mist comes down and halts the journey through the Highlands as the two main characters approach the village, who then sleep and wake up before entering the village for the first time, is present too in *Brigadoon*. A telephone kiosk links a visitor to the 'old country' back to the city, and to reality, in *I Know Where I'm Going*. Like these films, *Local Hero* uses repeated motifs – lights in the sky, the image of the rabbit, the telephone box – to build a sense of wonder and amazement.

Another influence came from television. During the writing of his script, Forsyth remembered *The Beverly Hillbillies*, an American situation comedy that had been extremely popular in America and the UK in the 1970s. The sitcom dealt with the clash between different cultures, when the Clampetts, a farming family from the traditionally poor rural Ozark Mountain region in the south eastern United States, move to the fabulously wealthy area of Beverly Hills in Los Angeles after oil is discovered on their land. As in *Local Hero*, the supposedly backward farmers frequently outwit the more sophisticated characters, who scheme constantly to deprive the Clampetts of their wealth. It appealed to Forsyth because its themes of displacement, difference and reversal were similar to the story he was trying to come up with in his new script.

The later critical attitude towards *Local Hero*, which compared it to *Whisky Galore!*, *The Maggie* and *Brigadoon*, was not always flattering (see Section 10). But critics missed the point of both *Brigadoon* and these other films, and of Forsyth's lasting vision and his great leap forward for cinema in this country. *Local Hero* is a story that constructs a view of Scotland drawn from contemporary events and from a strong tradition of Scottish narratives, where an affectionate portrait of Scotland is seen through the eyes of a visitor, the dramatic landscape is present as a character in the narrative, and the conflict of ideas between past and present, between tradition and modernity is played out against an idyll of Highland life. A misty, mystical picture of a village community is drawn with the obligatory ceilidh thrown in. And yet the film also creates a uniquely modern view, turning audience expectations around to show a familiar story from a different angle. Forsyth's earlier successes, and the keen interest of the press in the production, meant that the film carried the burden of being an almost unique example of a national cinema (see Section 10), but in fact it both acknowledged its origins and made something completely new.

The carefully honed cameo scenes in Forsyth's script are woven into a narrative, drawn from reality, which creates a fantastically humane narrative, warm and funny but also tinged with melancholy and regret. In its tone it looks back to its influences, but it also creates something original. A film of its time, it is also timeless. It could not have been made after the invention of the mobile phone, but its themes are still with us today (see Section 8).

5. *LOCAL HERO*: LANGUAGE AND *MISE-EN-SCÈNE*

Like every film, *Local Hero* uses a mixture of technology and effects to tell its story. The way in which the visuals and sound are used to tell the story of a film is known as its **language**. Film language can be extremely complex and technical. Camera angle, the distance between the camera and its subject and the ways in which the camera can move or be moved are all factors that contribute to how filmmakers, especially directors, make the visual aspect of their films tell the story. Similarly, the sound used in a film, although often overshadowed by the images, makes a crucial contribution to its effect and its impact on an audience.

The camera

A camera can film its subject from below or above. Filming from above (high angle) can make the thing being filmed – a character, for example – look small, vulnerable or menaced. Conversely, filming from below (low angle) can make the subject look big, powerful or dominant. A famous example of this latter case is the way the Italian dictator Mussolini, a small man, insisted that any photographs taken of him had to be from a low angle, to emphasise his power and strength, as well as making him look taller than he was.

All photographers taking a picture also have to decide how far away or how close to stand from their subject. In a moving narrative such as a film, where camera distance changes from one shot to the next, and the flow of these changes creates much of the film's narrative, how and where the camera stands in relation to its subject in each shot becomes crucial, as it actually 'tells' the story. Different distances are known as shots, and certain ones have been given names so that they can be described on storyboards (for example, the Long Shot, where we can see an entire figure and much of the background, or the Close Up, where we see just a person's face). Each of these shots produces a different effect and can be used in a variety of different ways within a film.

The camera can also move or be moved. There is a distinction between two kinds of movement. In the first sort, the camera can be swivelled or focussed in such a way as to make a single shot change. **Pan** is when a camera moves from right to left or left to right or up and down to show, perhaps, something huge and magnificent, such as a panoramic landscape. **Zoom**, when the focal length of the lens is changed so that the shot moves in closer to the subject, can be used to emphasise, for example, the shock and surprise on someone's face when something horrifying happens.

The camera can also be moved physically. A **tracking** shot is when the camera rests on a dolly truck that moves along a track producing an effect of steady movement. A **crane** shot is, obviously, a shot taken from the top of a moving crane. A **helicopter** shot is also what it says, a shot taken from a helicopter. Films with big budgets often open with a helicopter shot, showing a city skyline or a wild landscape to give an impression of scale, and to show from the start that this is a big film dealing with an important subject or a spectacular adventure.

Other camera shots have been developed since *Local Hero*'s time. (A **Bodycam** shot is where the camera is strapped to the cameraman's body, allowing it to move without wobbling or shaking, while shots produced on **Handheld** cameras, which do wobble, shake and move quickly, can create a feeling of authenticity, informality or anxiety.) But when Bill Forsyth was making his film in Pennan, film cameras were still large, expensive pieces of equipment that used celluloid film to record their subjects.

To analyse how the camera is used, it is useful to draw a small part of it frame by frame, in the same way as a storyboard – a shot-by-shot, scene-by-scene series of drawings of the entire film – is produced before a film is made. Although this has to some extent changed with the advent of digital technology, the reason for this approach is to ensure a film is completely planned before expensive technology needs to be hired and used. The entire visual and aural language of the film (including many more elements than the use of cameras and microphones, such as the lighting, the costumes, the props, the editing and the acting), all amounting to its *mise-en-scène*, can be worked out in advance, and so reduce the chances of costly mistakes.

Mise en scene: a storyboard

There is one scene in *Local Hero* that is especially famous, seeming to encapsulate as it does both the film's eerily haunting atmosphere and the unexpected and unusual twists in its story. It comes as Mac and Gordon accompany Ben to his shack after the beachcomber has revealed that he has no intention of selling the beach. Standing peeling some oranges Ben has given them, the American negotiator and the Scottish lawyer suddenly realise they are not alone. What happens next constitutes one of the film's dramatic climaxes, and its most memorable visual moment.

It is worth looking at part of this scene in detail, using a storyboard, in order to see how camera shots, music, sound and other aspects of *mise-en-scene* come together to create this striking piece of film.

Frame 1

Camera: Long Shot.
Action: As dusk falls, the villagers stream onto the beach in the distance.
Music: An ominous note sounds.
Dialogue: GORDON URQUHART: Oh-oh.

Camera: Mid Shot.
Action: Mac and Gordon Urquhart stop peeling the fruit
and look up.
Music: The ominous note continues.
Dialogue: URQUHART: They've taken the church road.

Camera: Long Shot.
Action: More and more of the villagers appear on the beach.
Music: The ominous note continues.

Frame 4

Camera: Close Up.
Action: Mac and Gordon stare anxiously at the villagers.
Music: The ominous note continues.
Dialogue: MAC: Maybe they just want to talk to him.
URQUHART: Think that's all they'll do?
MAC: Oh, sure. They just want to talk to him.

Frame 5.1

Camera: Mid Shot.
Action: The villagers are walking along the beach in the foreground with the sea and sunset in the background.
Music: The ominous note continues
Dialogue: MAC: There's an awful lot of them.
URQUHART: Yeah.

Camera: Mid Shot.
Action: A light appears in the sky on the horizon.
Music: The ominous note rises and changes to a choral chord of wonder.

Camera: Close Up.
Action: Mac and Gordon Urquhart stare at the light, wondering what it is.
Music: The music swells with a church organ adding to it.

Frame 7.1

Camera: Mid Shot, the camera tracking along the beach behind the villagers.
Action: The villagers slow as the light moves across the horizon.
Music: The choral chord of wonder continues.

Frame 7.2

Camera: Mid Shot.
Action: The villagers stop as the light changes direction and starts heading towards the beach.
Music: The choral chord of wonder continues.

Frame 8

Camera: Close Up.
Action: Mac and Gordon Urquhart exchange a wondering glance.
Music: The choral chord of wonder continues.

Frame 9

Camera: Long Shot.
Action: The light approaches the shore until it can be seen to be a helicopter searchlight.
Music: The choral chord of wonder continues.

Frame 10

Camera: Close Up.
Action: Mac and Gordon Urquhart are joined by Oldsen.
They all stare at the light.
Music: The choral chord of wonder continues.

Frame 11

Camera: Mid Shot.
Action: The helicopter descends until it seems to be coming
down on top of us. Its light fills the screen.
Music: The choral chord of wonder continues.

Camera: Close Up.
Action: Mac, Gordon and Oldsen stare at this mysterious
arrival from another world.
Music: The choral chord of wonder continues.

The visual language of *Local Hero*

Close examination of the shots in *Local Hero* reveals that,
in fact, the camerawork in the film is mostly conservative.
Although there is a helicopter shot in the film, when Mac
leaves Ferness and looks down regretfully to see Stella
hanging out her washing, it is used, as with every other shot
in the film, to emphasise the close interplay of character, not
to bring out a feeling of grandeur. The camera does not zoom
on any occasion, and most shots are static. There are exceptions to this, but in each of these the camera movement is
used mostly to show the actions or reactions of characters.

For example, when Mac and Oldsen visit Geddes's laboratory, and Marina, the beautiful scientist takes off her lab
coat and hands it to Oldsen before diving into the water,
the camera swings round onto Oldsen's and Mac's faces as
they watch her approach the water. The camera movement
is there to stress the attraction the two male characters feel
for her, and to bring out the comedy of two young men jointly
attracted to the same female. Similarly, when Mac meets
Oldsen in Aberdeen airport, he at first walks past Oldsen,

who has hidden the notice saying he is from Knox Oil, then walks back. As he returns, the camera follows him. The camera movement is used to highlight the comic misunderstanding between the characters.

Thus, although Forsyth does use the usual language of mid shots and close ups to bring out the comic moments, he and his technical team – the 'crew' responsible for the capturing Forsyth's vision – deliberately keep the acting and the dialogue to the fore in each scene, rather than distract the audience from them with technical wizardry.

Forsyth Hardy (Hardy, 171–208) has written of 'the two Bills', who both made significant contributions to Scottish films but in very different ways; and other critics too have commented on the differences between these two key figures in the creation of a Scottish screen industry. Bill Douglas, the first of these, used hardly any script for his trilogy of films called *My Childhood*, his masterpiece, relying solely on direction in the making of the film. Bill Forsyth, on the other hand, brought a polished script to the production, and filmed it. He was greatly assisted in this by Chris Menges, the Lighting Cameraman, whose job it was to develop a camera style that would bring out the best features of the film. The point here is that Forsyth's visuals rely entirely on the script, using only minimal camera direction, while Douglas created a completely new and original visual style, using nothing more than some notes and an intense and highly idiosyncratic manner of working with actors and the camera. Forsyth has thought out and planned everything in advance (although the unearthly shot of the helicopter coming in over the sea was not deliberate, and was taken spontaneously by the cameraman as he saw the remarkable sight – see Section 5, above), and has carefully and methodically crafted it, line by line. The careful timing of each little interchange gives it a feeling akin to tenderness, creating in the audience a kind of intimate, emotional involvement with the characters that is unique to Forsyth's films.

The bittersweet comedy, or comic sadness which predominates in Forsyth's film, is enhanced by the relatively constrained directing style. Nothing is allowed to deflect the viewer from the film's central point, which was also the reason Forsyth had W.H. Davies's lines printed on the front cover of the script. No flashy camerawork, special effect or swift editing was to interrupt or distract the audience from the subtle and intricate comedy of the characters' journey towards discovery and loss.

The sound
Sound is often overlooked in films. We can remember vivid action sequences or spectacular camerawork, but we are much less conscious of the sounds that accompany them. But it is nevertheless one of the most important ways of affecting an audience, perhaps all the more so because it acts on their unconscious rather than conscious minds.

Sound in films can be used in a variety of ways. Dialogue, music, additional sound effects and even silence can all be used to bring additional meaning to an image or to add atmosphere. But all sounds can be considered in one of two ways: *diegetic* and *non-diegetic*. Diegetic is when a sound is actually taking place in a narrative, such as a radio playing in the background of a domestic scene. Non-diegetic is when a sound is used which is not taking place in the story, such as the use of background music or an added-in sound effect.

The aural language of *Local Hero*
While many films use all these kinds of sounds lavishly to create a whole tapestry behind a film, colouring and deepening its emotional impact from start to finish, in *Local Hero* Bill Forsyth, as with the visuals, takes a minimal approach. It is as if he has deliberately decided not to employ all the tools at his disposal, or to use them only to support the dialogue, the characters and the comedy. Again, this stripped-down style of directing focuses on the script, allowing full concentration on the moments of realisation, the small comic epiphanies where something is revealed, either to a character or the audience.

For example, the sound at the beginning of the film is entirely diegetic – it is happening within the film, and is not added to the background to create meaning or atmosphere.

As the film begins we see Mac's beloved Porsche making its way through downtown freeway traffic and hear country music and an American voice telling us the weather, traffic conditions and the stock market reports. It is the radio in Mac's car, which acts as the opening music for the film. In the Knox Building, as Mac chats to his colleagues about his forthcoming visit to Scotland, some sounds are added in that background, but again these are diegetic, as in the noise of phones ringing. When Happer talks to his psychologist and dismisses him, we hear soft mood-music, or muzak, playing in the corridor outside his office. We hear it again as Mac, summoned to ascend to the offices at the top of the skyscraper, tentatively approaches Happer's secretary as she answers the phone to the British Prime Minister (then Margaret Thatcher). The muzak is diegetic again: it is not there to enhance the scene but is a realistic part of it.

Non-diegetic sound is still absent as the film develops. As Mac flies to Scotland the pilot's voice can be heard in the background making announcements. In Aberdeen airport, a voice is heard making announcements over the tannoy. These sound effects are part of the action. In fact, it is not until almost a quarter of the way into the film, just before Mac and Oldsen, as they drive north, encounter a mysterious mist, that non-diegetic sound is heard for the first time, with a short burst of atmospheric music which suggests that something mysterious, and different from what the characters (and probably the audience) expect, is about to happen. And it is not until the mist passes and the two men drive on the following morning that the film's musical soundtrack, the theme music composed by Mark Knofler of the band Dire Straits, begins.

The soundtrack: Mark Knopfler and *Local Hero*

Mark Knopfler was known at the time as the leader and main musical force of his chart-topping band Dire Straits, and it was David Puttnam's idea to bring him on board the film. Forsyth has stated that if anyone is owed a debt for the success of *Local Hero* it is Knofler for the impact his music had and the way it helped promote and market the film.

A film soundtrack, of course, has a great deal to do with the way the visuals on the screen work, but it also assists the launch and distribution of a film if it becomes a hit. Contemporary films rely on their music for their advertising and marketing to such an extent that they almost require a central song to be a hit, and this has certainly been the case for many recent films. Celine Dion's *My Heart Will Go On*, which was the key musical moment in the film *Titanic*, illustrates how the success of a major film is assisted by the use of a number one hit, and how that success feeds in turn into the career of the musical performer. Indeed we could say that today the music and film industries partner each other to create stars, fame and commercial success in both fields. But at the time of *Local Hero*, this kind of cross-media work was in its earliest days, and was associated more with Hollywood blockbusters, not small British-made films, and certainly not Scottish ones.

Forsyth was surprised to learn that Knopfler, an artist usually associated with the North-East of England, had been born in Glasgow and had spent most of his childhood there. He was impressed too by the way Knopfler liked the film, wanted to assist with a Scottish-made project and identified with the *Local Hero*'s message and themes. He felt that the music the guitarist composed brought out the film's strengths, contributing depth and an eerie, memorable atmosphere that added something crucial to the production. As described earlier, Knopfler and his band joined the production during the ceilidh scene, some of the Dire Straits members, such as keyboardist Alan Clark (who is the piano player in the film) appearing with the Ace Tones on stage, to allow Forsyth to weave the music into the action (see Section 3). Other musicians involved included Gerry Rafferty, who sang the vocal on Knopfler's song *The Way It Always Starts* on the album of the sound track (Perrone).

Even so, Knopfler's soundtrack, like all non-diegetic sound in the film, is used sparingly, and in a particular way. Forsyth carefully and skilfully builds it through the film. It lasts for less than a minute as Oldsen and Mac arrive in Ferness, and is not heard again until after Mac has made his first phone call to America only to be cut off from his colleague Cal. As Mac comes out of the telephone box – which acts as a kind of magical gateway between worlds – and stands staring up at the sky, the haunting sound track is heard again. Again, it lasts only for a few minutes. In fact, Knopfler's music is used consistently by Forsyth at important moments during Mac's development to represent the way the beautiful scenery and the atmosphere of Ferness are working on him, gradually changing him from hard-headed negotiator to aimless and happy wanderer. As the movie unfolds the sound track tells us at critical points that Mac is undergoing a transformation, that the mysterious and magical qualities of the environment are working their effect, penetrating his hard American shell and reshaping him from within. Built into the music is a well-known traditional Gaelic song, *Chi ma na morbheanna/The Mist-Covered Mountains*, composed by Cameron of Ballachullish, which is used at particularly poignant moments in the film. It is a song of exile, where the traveller sees Glencoe and other scenes from his earlier life in his mind's eye. It is first heard in the film where the sea washes over Mac's watch, and again at the ceilidh. The use of a piece of music so redolent of longing and loss adds further to the soundtrack's mood. Used increasingly through the film until its end, when the phone ringing in the telephone box tells us that Mac wants to return, the entire musical theme is only played from start to end as the final credits come up, mirroring the development of the central character and so contributing a crucial dimension to the film's narrative.

Apart from Knopfler's score, which is as haunting as the film's images and so strongly associated with them that, like all the best theme music, it is inseparable from the work it was composed for, almost every other sound in *Local Hero* is diegetic. Even the music played by the Ace Tones at the ceilidh is real: it has not been dubbed, edited or enhanced in any way.

So in terms of film language and the resulting *mise-en-scène* (meaning, the way everything is placed in the scene to bring out film's visual meaning), Forsyth seems not to want to show us a fictional world of dizzying camera shots and

emotive sound. He does not set out to dazzle us with specta-
cle. Instead, he wants to let us see and hear the world as it
really is. He takes, in fact, a highly documentary approach to
fictional filmmaking.

6. *LOCAL HERO*:
NARRATIVE

Narrative in film means everything to do with the story. It is one of the main ways we analyse a film, and it resembles the ways in which we analyse literary texts such as poems and novels. Things such as the characters, their motivation, the order of events, the text's structure, its tone, its imagery, its themes and any other way of understanding how the story is told by looking at it in detail, are relevant here.

There have been many theorists whose work has been important to the study of narrative. Aristotle was the first to coin the term *catharsis*, a word we still use to today to mean a beneficial burning out of emotion in an audience. He also described functions of character, especially the protagonist (the chief character or characters) and the antagonist (the opposing character or force). Later theorists brought other insights. Vladimir Propp showed that many stories share stock characters and stock events. Tzetsan Todorov demonstrated that many stories pass through recognisable phases. Roland Barthes argued that texts were coded in ways an audience could interpret, while the structuralist Claude Levi-Strauss observed that myths had much to do with opposites and the tensions that resulted from them.

Other commentators belong more to the world of practice. Screenwriting gurus rather than academic theorists, they take a practical approach. Syd Field bases his ideas entirely on structure (generally, this is true of all Hollywood script advisers). Robert McKee stresses the importance of an event near the start of the story which he calls the Inciting Incident. Another influential script adviser, Christopher Vogler, bases his theory on the mythologist Joseph Campbell (in turn a follower of Jung), and sees a screenplay as a kind of psychological map, with key roles played at important moments by mythic figures such as Threshold Guardians, Shapeshifters, Shadows, Mentors and others.

All of these theories are much more complex than described here, and it should be borne in mind that none of them claim to explain fully screenwriting or any other kind of story telling. We should always remember that any rules or patterns regarding narrative have been drawn from the observation of stories rather than the other way round: there are no golden rules, only a few principles. And we can always find exceptions to these, as we are constantly in search of new ways to depict the world we live in and the ones we imagine. And ultimately, perhaps we should bear in mind the words of another Hollywood practitioner, William Goldman, when he writes about the many 'insights' people in the film industry claim to have into what makes films work: 'Nobody knows anything'.

Narrative theory and *Local Hero*

What does all this mean to analysing *Local Hero*?

To some extent we can see all these theories in Forsyth's film, but it is also clear that none of them really explain it. There is a protagonist – Mac, played by Peter Riegert – but the antagonist is less clear. Probably it is the capitalist force that affects everyone's life – Happer, Mac, the village – seeming to bring great wealth but in reality benefiting no-one. Part of the opposing force also seems to be Ben, who stays on the beach no matter what amount of money Mac offers him, but the benign beachcomber is hardly a negative figure. Although we could argue that Mac is a stock figure, it is hard to find Propp's other elements in the film. The story does pass through recognisable phases, but this very sweeping model does not allow any close analysis. In fact, when we try to apply any of these theoretical approaches, we can see that while some aspects of *Local Hero* do conform to them, they do not help us to grasp the particular nature of the film. At best (as with all other dramas) they help us understand only a tiny part of it.

Local Hero seems to follow the principles of the screen-writing gurus even less. We can perhaps find a three-act structure, an Inciting Incident and characters who play mythic roles conducting us through major turning points in the drama, but it is also clear that the film operates in different ways from these overarching models. Its narrative structure simply does not follow the shape recommended by

these practitioners. (Despite this, the film was to be criticised for its closeness to Hollywood traditions, as opposed to
Forsyth's earlier films – see Section 10).

Local Hero, although it does follow one linking character
and explores large themes, does not just describe a hero's
journey, despite its title. A comedy, it explores not so much
the lessons of experience or the overcoming of challenges,
but the fact that experience sometimes teaches us little,
that we are who we are under our many pretensions and
ambitions, full of frailties and flaws, and that we often go
on repeating the same mistakes. Looked at closely, we can
see that the film's structure (the master element beloved
of the Hollywood script doctors) is much looser than they
advise: deliberately manipulated, in fact, to allow for many
small scenes, all of them relevant, all of them comic. These
moments may be miniatures but they make an important
contribution to the film; in fact, in their own way they are
just as important to the story as Mac's un-heroic journey
to Scotland and back again. Happer's futile relationship
with his psychologist, the villagers' eccentric conversations
and behaviour, the moment at the ceilidh where Mac tells
Gordon he wants to swap places with him, the scene where
Ben explains to Mac why he won't sell the beach, may all be
vignettes – or tiny portraits – but they are given great prominence. They do not just assist the central story: they are
important discoveries in themselves. Indeed, as Mac's quest
to buy the village and beach develops, he becomes increasingly involved in these distractions, and as a result notices
more and more of the strange world around him, as if the
value of smallness and awareness of the extraordinary existence of ordinary things is one of the film's central concepts.
Similarly, repeated images of everyday surroundings underscore Mac's journey. The insistence on the natural beauty
of the landscape, for example, the play of the Northern
Lights against the Scottish sky, the repeated motif of the
telephone box, the sea with its human persona of Marina
and the rural setting, all have an impact on Mac and on the
audience. These things are timeless, untamed, elemental:
they are to be respected rather than sold like commodities,

which is the point Ben makes as he lifts the handful of sand
and asks Mac to give him a pound for every grain of it. Ben
knows that Mac does not understand what he is trying to
acquire. The thoughtlessness of money, and its inability to
bring any benefit – to 'look after' the beach, as Ben describes
it – is made clear. As these moments and many others occur,
the audience becomes increasingly aware that Forsyth's
'message' (although it is put with great charm and lightness) is that important things like the environment, happiness and belonging cannot be bought. Ben laughs as Mac and
Urquhart ask him how much the beach is worth: he knows
it is not for sale. And as Mac experiences these moments
of clarity he changes, growing aware that there are much
more important things than money and a career. He leaves
the village, having been dismissed from it by Happer, his
function done, and returns to Houston. The last shot shows
the film's most iconic image, the red telephone box, ringing
in the village. Mac is trying to 'phone home'.

   Local Hero does not, in fact, use the same approach to telling
its story as more traditionally Hollywood-based Scottish films,
such as the 1996 version of *Rob Roy* (Manderson, 44) directed
by Michael Caton-Jones and starring Liam Neeson, which
can be clearly seen to follow the traditional three-act structure recommended by the screenwriting advisers. Instead,
it takes a much more meandering route towards its subject
matter, looking for comic moments, subtle and unexpected
interplay between characters, and images and events that
provide epiphanies in characters' souls. Forsyth, as outlined
earlier, looked for his inspiration less to Hollywood than to
different traditions such as the British one of the Ealing
comedies (see Section 4). But he was also inspired by the
French comedies of Jacques Tati and other European traditions where the point is not necessarily a forceful, forward-
driving story, but something much more ironic, subtle and
nuanced.

   In *Local Hero*, the Hollywood model of a controlling structure is replaced by another approach. This is not to say
that we cannot analyse character, themes, plot and so on in
the same way as in a Hollywood film, but it does mean that

the relative weight of these elements is not the same as the American tradition. We should therefore understand and appreciate *Local Hero* as something rather different from the most dominant form of Western cinema.

7. *LOCAL HERO*: CHARACTERS

Mac: 'We have an injured rabbit also.'

Mac is the character we see throughout the film, whose geographical and spiritual journey we follow and whose character development or 'arc' makes up the central trajectory of the film. He is clearly the protagonist: the mythical figure who sets out on a quest; and in many ways he can be considered the "hero" of the story, albeit a rather confused and hapless one.

We first meet Mac in his daily life in Houston, Texas, driving his Porsche to his place of work. He is a negotiator, working for a conglomerate to buy up areas of the world where oil might be found. His office in Knox Oil & Gas is a glass and steel box high up in a skyscraper. Through the windows he can look into the other glass boxes at his colleagues, or at other skyscrapers that surround his own. It is telling that, although he can see these people through the glass, he finds it hard to actually meet and talk to them, and can only do so by phone. He phones his work colleague Cal to ask him to lunch, but has to ask twice: Cal does not seem especially keen. Later, when Mac phones from Scotland to say how he is, Cal is unmoved when Mac is cut off. Similarly, after Mac has been told he has to go to Scotland to buy Ferness, he phones a female colleague in an adjacent office to ask her out. She refuses.

Mac is alone. He has no friends, no ties with anyone. His ex-wife, whom he phones from his apartment after being told he is to go to Scotland, argues with him. He seems successful, with an excellent salary, an executive's job, a Porsche and 'over fifty thousand dollars in securities', but his life is empty. He seems unaware of this at the start of the film, outwardly content with his lot, or at least resigned to it. But that will change.

As Mac tunes in to the rhythms of a tiny town on the Scottish coast, to its ever-changing tides and skies, his behaviour alters. At first he is uneasy and out of place. He asks Gordon Urquhart the hotel manager and town lawyer for an adapter to charge his briefcase, and has to endure Gordon and Stella's mockery for it. But gradually he seems to relax. He starts to chat to people rather than be businesslike.

MAC: Working hard?
RODDY: Fixing creels. Trying to keep the lobsters in and the crabs out.
MAC: What do you do with the lobsters?
RODDY: They catch a plane every night to Inverness. Next day they're being eaten in London or Paris. Oh aye, they see the world.
MAC: Don't you eat them?
RODDY: Oh no, too expensive.
MAC: Do you work here as well as the bar?
RODDY: Oh aye, we all muck in together. Do every job that's needing done.
ALL: Aye.
JONATHAN: Have you only got one job?
MAC: *(sheepish)* Yeh, just one.
IAIN: How's the telephone box. Is it all right for you?
MAC: Great.
IAIN: Gideon's going to give it a fresh coat of paint.
MAC: Great.
GIDEON: Any particular colour you'd like?
MAC: Red's alright. Cord could be a little longer though. In America cords are longer.
>
> *Pause*

Whose baby?
> *Everyone looks away*

The eccentricities of the small town – the single dog permanently barring its single road, old Gideon forever painting the boat and changing its name, the repair to the hotel roof that never seems to finish, and the chat of the groups of locals who hang about the pier – begin to alter him. So does the environment: he starts to wander by the sea rather than walking purposefully, noticing shells and crabs and seaweed. He notices the sky too, as Happer has told him to do, but he also falls under its spell: the movement of the stars and the

Northern Lights and meteors. While the locals take the sky
and the stars for granted, Mac (and Happer, when Mac talks
to him on the telephone) is awed by it.

Mac's development from sharp businessman to shore
wanderer continues. He has earlier told Oldsen about the
electronic alarm on his watch (during the same conversation, as they both wait in the car after the mist has come
down, he proudly shows Oldsen a picture of his Porsche).
As he becomes more and more acclimatised to the spell of
the Scottish landscape, he forgets his watch and leaves it
bleeping ineffectively on a stone. Soon he has exchanged
his suit for an old pullover and tatty trousers. His changed
appearance is matched by his behaviour. He no longer cares
about negotiating or getting the right price for the town, the
beach or the bay. He brings shells back to the hotel from
the rock pools and cleans them in the sink in his room, in
contrast now to the locals, and to Victor, the Russian trawler
man, who sits downstairs with Gordon Urquhart calculating
his stock market investments. Mac is more interested in the
shells, their shapes and colours and smells, than anything
else (and so is Oldsen, whose character arc mirrors Mac's).
At the ceilidh, wandering around drunk and smiling, Mac
refuses to negotiate with Gordon Urquhart even for a joke.
He is no longer interested: what he wants is contentment
and belonging. He even offers to swap lives with Gordon. But
he insists that Gordon leaves his wife Stella with him. It is
typical of Gordon Urquhart that, drunken and light-hearted
conversation though this is, he accepts Mac's offer.

By the last third of the film, Mac has become an accepted
part of the town. He is unshaven, aimless and happy, entirely
used to the pace and beauty of the place. He has changed so
much he is literally unrecognisable. When Happer arrives
unexpectedly he mistakes the neater Oldsen for his employee.
When Mac identifies himself Happer can't believe it. 'Are *you*
MacIntyre?' he asks incredulously.

From the moment Happer lands Mac changes again: forced
to return, in fact, to the man he has been before he arrived
in the village. Happer orders him to leave right away: the
multi-millionaire no longer has any need for him in Scotland.

Instead, Happer turns to Oldsen, who now becomes the trusted on-site adviser that Mac has been. Happer dismisses Mac with '... and MacIntyre – get a shave.' Mac is reduced to the commodity he was at the start of the film, out of place, friendless, and belonging nowhere, but he is no longer unaware of it.

During the film's last scenes, Mac reverts to what he was at the start of the film: he dons his smart suit, shaves and brushes his hair, and bids Gordon Urquhart farewell. As he flies off he sees, from the glass and steel cabin of the helicopter, Stella, his real love, hanging out her tights on the washing line. He hasn't said goodbye. She smiles mysteriously up at him as she watches him leave. As the helicopter thrums overhead, the village worthies mark his passing.

> PETER: Is that the Yank in that thing, Edward?
> EDWARD: Aye Peter, that's him away.
> PETER: Ah bugger it. I meant to say cheerio.

Mac's departure, as so often in Forsyth's films, is treated ambiguously: the local people might care about him and want him to return, but equally they might not (see Section 3).

As he arrives back in Houston, it is as if he has never been away. His apartment is neat, empty and impersonal, with a view from the window over the city. He pulls the shells from his pocket and hauls back the window to go out on his terrace. Below him lies the great city, with its police sirens and skyscrapers. Mac's journey is over, his character arc complete. He has changed and yet returned to where he began. His story is over – unless he decides to return to where his heart is.

Felix Happer: 'I like this place. The air is good, clear.'

Felix Happer is the owner of Knox Oil & Gas, a conglomerate bought from the Knox family by his father. He is an older man who lives alone and who, despite his great wealth, seems more interested in watching the movement of the planets than running his business. When we first see him, he is asleep during a meeting of his directors, who continue in whispers around him. Happer seems not to care about his company or its acquisitions, and it seems that the business could run just as well without him.

Happer's office at the top of the Knox building is devoted to the stars. In fact, Happer's character is linked with the sky throughout, as if he is a star or a planet himself, something that ordinary mortals such as Mac cannot ever control or become. His godlike status is emphasised by the way people treat him. His directors whisper through a meeting rather than wake him, his employees jump to obey him, and important people queue to talk to him.

SECRETARY: Ask his Serene Highness to call back in half an hour.

Nevertheless, Happer is not happy. In fact, his mental health is not good. He is paying a therapist, Moritz, to subject him to treatment that consists of insulting him. The therapy soon gets out of hand, Moritz threatening to tie Happer up, subjecting him to abusive phone calls and finally spelling an insulting message on the penthouse office window. But early in the film Moritz puts his finger, perhaps inadvertently, on Happer's problem, asking the older man if he has ever wanted a family and a home. This draws a reaction from the millionaire. 'Did you really mean that?' 'Hell, no, look at me, Mr Happer. I'm a single man,' the therapist answers, as if that would reassure anyone. But it is the moment when we see through Happer's shell to what is really troubling him.

Other glimpses reveal a man who for all his power and wealth lives in similar way to Mac. He lives alone and appears to have no close relationships. His interest in the stars and the planets is obsessive and intense, as if his hobby is a substitute for much else.

But to the rest of the world Happer is a figure like a god, or very close to one, and this is emphasised by how and where he appears. (It may also refer, with characteristic dryness on Forsyth's part, to the presence of Burt Lancaster, a major Hollywood star, in a homespun Scottish movie, where, as Forsyth has stated, the interest and participation of a major movie star had previously been unthinkable.) (Forsyth, 2008) Happer's office is at the top of the skyscraper, reached only by a single flight of open stairs. His office and his secretary's are full of planetary objects: globes, orbs and sceptres, all rendered in the same smooth steel. He seems as strange and wonderful as a god, insisting that Mac phone him with reports on the sky, and that he should 'keep his eye on Virgo'. Later, when Mac does phone him with reports of the night sky from Furness, his excitement at the appearance of the Northern Lights is palpable.

One of the most stunning moments in the film is when the villagers walk along the beach to deal with Ben, the beachcomber. We fear the worst for the elderly man as they approach his shack: there is menace in their silence and purposefulness. As they walk against the background of a red sunset what looks like a star, but brighter and lower, appears. It moves rapidly along the skyline and then swings in. Is it a planet come down to earth? A god come to intercede on Ben's behalf? As it reaches the shore we see it is a helicopter, bringing Happer to Furness (see Section 5). Visually, it is a stunning moment, as if a star has indeed landed in this most unlikely of places (see Section 4).

Deus ex machina is a dramatic term which usually means a poor piece of theatrical business where a convenient bit of plot is introduced at the end of a drama to explain everything away. It means literally 'god out of a machine', because it originates from a classical Greek and Roman theatrical practice where a god would suddenly appear in a chariot at the end of a tragedy and solve all the dramatic problems. But in *Local Hero* this device is literal, the divine figure of Felix Happer (and Burt Lancaster) arriving to provide the solution. And in fact Happer does solve the problem, with Ben's help. Magically, the environment is saved, the villagers get their money, or some of it, the beach is unspoilt and everybody, except Mac, gets what he or she wants. It is as if Forsyth plays here with the concept of *Deus ex machina* and finds within what is generally considered a clumsy dramatic device a unique and original approach. It is a characteristically brilliant and humorous piece of Forsythian trickery.

Ben Knox: 'If you got your hands on the place it would be bye-bye beach forever.'

Ben Knox, played by Fulton MacKay, appears less in the film than Mac, Oldsen or Gordon Urquhart, but he is a hugely significant character. In terms of his function within the screenplay, he balances Happer, providing an equal but different kind of force to the billionaire's godlike power. While Happer represents the sky, Ben is the land, especially the beach, and he is prepared to defend it with all his tenacity against the oil business.

Ben is a beachcomber. He lives by collecting the debris washed up by the tide. The beach provides him with food (he offers Urquhart and Mac oranges found in a crate washed up on the beach, and tells the two men about the time he found a coconut); shelter (his hut is made of old crates, planks and an upturned boat); and work ('Everyone's got to work, Gordon'). He is not seen much at the start of the film, or for some way into the action; he is just a presence in the distance, as much a part of the background as the mountains or the sea. As Mac and Urquhart try to figure out just how much to pay for the bay and town, however, they go to Ben for advice. 'How much would you figure the beach is worth, Ben?' Mac asks. The elderly man doesn't answer, just laughs richly and shakes his head. 'How much is the beach worth? That's a good one.'

Ben seems like a harmless eccentric, but as the story unfolds he is revealed to be much more. Urquhart discovers that Ben legally owns the beach. Mac also learns that Ben's second name is Knox. Unlike Mac, with his fake Scottish surname, and Happer, whose father bought Knox Oil & Gas from Andrew Knox, Ben's link with his origins is authentic: he is living on exactly the same spot as his ancestors. There is even the possibility that Ben Knox is related to the original owner of the oil company. Mac, Urquhart and Victor, the Russian trawler man, go to see Ben at his hut again. They try to trick him, asking if he has proof that his family owns the beach. But as this scene develops, Ben reveals his real wisdom. Far from being tricked, he tricks them:

BEN: Right, would you give me a pound note for every grain
of sand I have in my hand? You can have the beach for that
... There, saved you a pound or two there.
MAC: Come on Ben. I didn't come here to play games. Let's
negotiate in a businesslike way.
BEN: Oh dear, oh dear. You could have had yourself a nice
purchase there, Mr MacIntyre. I couldn't hold more than
ten thousand grains of sand in my hand at a time ... Did
you think it would be a bigger number?
MAC: You took advantage of me, Ben.
BEN: Did I?

It is impossible for Mac, the townspeople, Gordon Urquhart
and Victor to believe that some things do not have a price.
Only Ben knows this, and he sticks to it. And he knows much
else that people do not give him credit for. Walking back with
Mac and Gordon Urquhart to his hut, he tells them some of
the beach's history.

URQUHART: What if I told you that four hundred, maybe
five hundred people could make their living right here, if
things were allowed to change?
BEN: Well it wouldn't be the first time, would it?
URQUHART: What do you mean?
BEN: Local history, Gordon. This beach used to be a good
living for three hundred people. Big business. Two hundred
years ago this beach was turning over fifteen thousand a
year. Then the trade routes opened up to the east and so –
farewell Ferness. The business went but the beach is still
here ...

Ben has endurance, history and integrity on his side. He
is the only one of the locals not prepared to sell the bay, but
he is the one that counts. He is in fact the 'local hero' of the
title, and it is not meant ironically. In the end, when Mac is
revealed as just another employee of a big company who can
be sent back to the States as easily as he has been ordered
to leave it, Gordon Urquhart as a profiteering lawyer who
always takes whatever deal is offered, and Happer as an

egotist easily flattered by the vision of an Institute named after himself, it is Ben who decides the real fate of the beach.

Danny Oldsen: 'Do you think Stella and Gordon do it every night?'

Oldsen, played by Peter Capaldi in his first screen role, is the naïve, awkward and gormless young man who meets Mac at Aberdeen airport and accompanies him through his quest in Furness. He like Mac is an employee of Knox Oil & Gas, and illustrates the fact that Scotland too can produce its own brand of lost young men. He is also like Mac and Happer in that he also has obsessive interests in things – in his case, languages (he can speak eleven, although Gaelic is not one of them) – but his talents fail to link him with his own culture or to fill the emptiness in his life.

What Oldsen is in search of, like Mac, is love. He is deeply interested in girls and thinks of almost nothing else. When he meets Marina, the marine biologist, at the research centre just after Mac's arrival, he finds the object of his desire. As she hands over her white coat and dives into the water in her sheer black swimsuit, he cannot take his eyes off her. His longing for her grows through the rest of the film, an attraction that becomes deeper as he, like Mac, loses touch with meaningless reality and tunes in to the rhythms of the tides. As he becomes more intimate and familiar with Marina, kissing her legs and then her feet, he finds her toes are webbed. As always in a film by Forsyth the moment seems ambiguous, a flash of the impossible in the midst of the real. We cannot be certain how realistic or fantastic it is meant to be.

> OLDSEN: You taste salty.
> MARINA: You're on the fresh side.

Oldsen also provides moments of comedy throughout the film, representing a more foolish yet empathetic character than the sombre Mac. He is clumsy and clown-like, asking Mac if he can help him carry his baggage at Aberdeen airport and then only taking his coat; being pursued by the punk girl at the ceilidh; bringing back an order for roast beef sandwiches when asked to find out what Ben and Happer are talking about in the beachcomber's shack. And yet this portrait, typically of Forsyth, is gentle, leaving space for the character's essential likeability.

> MARINA: There's stuff fetching up here all the way from the Bahamas.
> OLDSEN: That's a long way.
> MARINA: Do you swim?
> OLDSEN: Not that far.

In terms of his function within the narrative, Oldsen acts as Mac's mirror, travelling along the same arc as Mac but in a more comic way, until the last phase of the drama, when his fate and Mac's suddenly cross over. As Mac is dismissed by Happer, ordered to return to the States, Oldsen steps forward to be taken into the millionaire's confidence. The sidekick has become the dominant force: Mac's status and self-esteem have suddenly been given to his foolish double. Oldsen also gets another thing Mac does not: the girl. In his last scene in the film, he pursues Marina into the water. She flips under the waves, revealing for just a second a mermaid's tail. Mac, in love with Stella, does not even say goodbye to her before he leaves. Oldsen, the hapless assistant, has won everything, and Mac has lost it.

Gordon Urquhart: 'Oh boy, we're going to be rich.'

Gordon Urquhart is the person in the film most interested in money, even more so than the mediator Mac and the wealthy Happer. He is completely focussed on it, to the exclusion of almost everything else, apart from his wife Stella. He has several jobs: hotel owner, town lawyer, and sometimes, as he tells Mac, taxi driver. He acts as the main point of contact between the townspeople and Mac, talking to them from the pulpit in the church while the local minister asks permission to say a prayer.

Mac is well aware of how important Urquhart is to the townsfolk's desire for cash. 'What do you make of Urquhart

then?' Oldsen asks Mac as they walk on the beach. 'He smells
the money,' Mac replies. If Happer represents the sky, and
Ben the land, Urquhart represents commerce. He has abso-
lutely no qualms about selling the beach, the bay and all
the properties in the village, and knows perfectly well that
the villagers will have none either. He himself will profit
hugely: the sale of the hotel will make him rich; and after
Mac and Oldsen leave his office he jumps onto his chair and
bounces up and down with a movement reminiscent of the
bumping noises made by him and Stella during the night in
their bedroom, and also like the incessant tapping made by
the repair man, Andrew, who never seems to finish his work
on the hotel roof. As the deal develops, Urquhart becomes
more and more important to it, skilfully steering the negotiation towards the highest possible amount for himself and
the other villagers. He helps the Russian Victor with his
stock market shares and seems to lead and advise the whole
village, organising the ceilidh, paying the band, and helping
Mac as they try to persuade Ben to change his mind. In fact,
his role in the village seems much more like the traditional
role of a minister than a lawyer, advising, counselling and
leading his flock: Forsyth's wry comment on how commerce
has become a god even in this remote place. In an ironic way,
Gordon could be a 'local hero' himself: certainly the village
would have regarded him as one if he had pulled the oil
refinery deal off.

But despite his enthusiasm for being rich, Urquhart is not a
villain. It would have been easy for Forsyth to have made him
that, and work the drama around a greedy lawyer prepared
to go to any lengths to sell the land only to be opposed by a
man of integrity. But Gordon Urquhart is not the real antagonist, although he may represent part of one. As a character he
is not cynical or especially unlikeable. Like Oldsen, Mac and
others, he comes across instead as rather innocent, simply
trying to get what he wants in a world that resists it. He
treat Mac's original request to buy the whole bay as almost
an intellectual exercise ('Well, you're talking about fifteen –
maybe twenty properties. You've got to be talking about a lot
of money.') But his behaviour when he jumps on the chair

after Mac leaves shows a different side: joyful, impish and playful. He has a sense of humour too, perhaps a little on the cruel side but still funny, as when he offers to send for the vet after Mac and Oldsen have eaten Trudi the rabbit. He is, in his own way, capable, skilful and trustworthy, with Victor and the whole of the village entrusting him with their financial affairs. He even has ethics. 'Shit, these are South African,' he says as he looks at the oranges Ben has given to him and Mac, referring to an anti-apartheid boycott of South African goods then in operation in the UK. Forsyth is, of course, poking fun at the type of person who can exploit others without a second thought but keeps his conscience clear by subscribing to liberal causes. Urquhart comes across as self-seeking and self-satisfied, but he is hardly a dark character.

But perhaps the main reason that Gordon Urquhart is not a villain, or someone we can condemn for having no redeeming characteristics, is because of the character he is most associated with: his wife Stella.

Stella: 'What lovely long eyelashes you've got.'

'Stella' is a name which means 'star', but Gordon Urquhart's wife has a much more earthy purpose. When we first meet her, she is in bed with her husband. As Mac lies awake, the rabbit Trudi twitching her whiskers at his side, the sound of love-making comes through the ceiling from upstairs. Stella and Urquhart have a vigorous and adventurous sex life, as Mac and Oldsen know from the start. 'Do you think Stella and Gordon do it every night?' Oldsen asks. 'Of course not,' Mac replies. But he is wrong. Stella and Gordon do it all the time, even during hotel lunch breaks.

> STELLA: What'll we get for Christmas this year?
> URQUHART: We could get that new mattress.

Stella represents sexuality, a strain of eroticism that Forsyth puts forward as part of the order of things, as much a part of nature as the sky, sea and land. She may even be a dryad or spirit, something alluring and desirable that Mac, as well as Gordon, lusts after, and probably loves. She is the earthbound equivalent of Marina, who, it is shown, is really a mermaid. In a drunken conversation with Gordon Urquhart after the ceilidh, Mac offers to swap places with Gordon, provided Urquhart is prepared to give up Stella. Mac loves Stella and would, by the end of the film, do anything to be with her. She acts as another way in which the place deeply affects him, changing him from within. But he is not destined to win his heart's desire.

Marina: 'This is my bay.'
Marina obviously represents the sea. We only see her near water, first meeting her at Geddes's laboratory as she dives in to repair an underwater valve. Later, she reappears unexpectedly at the shore's edge. Soon Oldsen, who is in love with her, understands that she will always come from the ocean.

Marina is a mermaid. She materialises suddenly and without warning, as if she does not quite belong to the real world, and she is a figure of certainty and some power. 'Come down! I want to talk to you!' she commands as Oldsen spies on her from behind a rock, thinking he is unobserved. Earlier in the film, as she walks away from Oldsen in the laboratory, having just dived in to save the tides, she gives him a knowing look over her shoulder, as if she realises the power of her attraction and knows exactly what is going on in his mind. In Ferness, she is equally calm about the sea and the way it will not be harmed when Oldsen tells her that the oil company plans to turn the bay into an oil refinery. She has a wisdom that is the equal of Ben's about the land.

Like Ben, Marina guards the environment, and she knows all about it: the flow of the Gulf Stream along the coast and the scientific causes of the Northern Lights. Like Ben, she protects the element she represents by giving richer, more powerful people ideas that flatter them or make them see different ways towards their plans. In the end, it is a combination of Marina's and Ben's ideas that Happer decides on, with a research institute dedicated to the study of the sea and the sky, possibly called 'The Happer Institute', to be established in the bay rather than the refinery. It is Oldsen who suggests it, but it is Marina who has given him the idea.

In fact, the female characters are given some prominence in the film. In cinema generally, the way female characters are represented or cast in dramas has been strongly criticised; the fact that smaller and fewer roles are written for women, and that scenes where they do appear almost inevitably link them with domesticity, sexuality or romantic love, is seen as a way in which cinematic representations perpetuate injustice. If women are constantly portrayed in stereotypical or subservient roles, it is argued, we are more likely to assume that is true. For the same reason, the film industry will always remain dominated by male actors if few lead roles are written for actresses.

While it is true that *Local Hero* does not break with this tradition entirely, it is also true that the characters of Stella and Marina are important to the film. In fact, they are equal and essential counterweights to the characters of Ben and Happer – and taken together these characters represent four natural elements: earth, sky, water and sexuality. The female characters are not there merely to be in the background. They do represent and enact male desire, but they use their powers consciously, like sirens, with Marina's knowledge of her control of Danny Oldsen and Stella's equally strong hold over her husband. As Mac signs the cheque for payment for his stay at the hotel, Urquhart tells him to make it out to Stella: 'She's the boss.'

In addition to this, the whole drama focuses around and stresses traditional female attitudes and attributes rather than male ones. Indeed, the traditionally masculine attributes of drive, ambition, success and achievement are criticised and deliberately eroded by Forsyth, replaced with the traditionally feminine values of relationships, love, tenderness and protection of what is vulnerable. In this way, Forsyth's values in *Local Hero* can from the outset be seen as much more feminine than masculine.

8. *LOCAL HERO*: THEMES

The environment

Forsyth has stated in recent interviews that the 'message' of the film *Local Hero* – if it has such a thing – is to do with the environment. But he adds that this element of the film is, to use his expression, 'sweet' rather than forceful (Forsyth, 2008), light rather than self-conscious. The preservation of the village, the beach and the beautiful landscape are the key issues in the film, but it is also an entertainment, a light-hearted and enjoyable experience rather than a lesson.

The choice between unspoiled natural beauty and economic gain were exactly the issues that were raised with the discovery and exploitation of North Sea Gas in the 1970s and 80s. Indeed, it was stories relating to the oil boom in Aberdeenshire that David Puttnam passed to Bill Forsyth when he was trying to encourage Forsyth to come up with a script for which Puttnam could raise a major budget (see Section 3).

The film starts with an urban landscape: the Houston freeway, as Mac drives to work. His office block existence is soulless, as is his apartment. Both are made of hard, shiny surfaces: glass, steel and tile. The soullessness continues after Mac arrives in Scotland, with the locations being an airport (in Aberdeen, but with the same impersonal appearance as an airport anywhere), and a laboratory where the landscape is reduced to a model, the Ice Age can be simulated and the tides can be reproduced by means of sensors – which fail:

> WATT: This could be the petro-chemical capital of the free world!
> GEDDES: Six months blasting, two years construction. It'll last a thousand years! Forever. It'll even survive the next Ice Age. We've proved that you know! We've proved it! We simulated ten thousand years of intense glaciation over the whole bay.
> WATT: Of course we don't *need* that Ice Age. We can divert the Gulf Stream and unfreeze the Arctic Circle. He proved

it right here. But they won't listen. They *want* to freeze.
GEDDES: Thank you Norman, but there was no need to
bring that up ...

But, as Mac and Oldsen head north for the town of Ferness,
the urban landscape disappears. Caught in a mysterious
mist and forced to sleep in the car overnight, they wake in
the morning to beautiful scenery. They have entered a different world.

Throughout the film, Forsyth makes it clear that the local
people by and large take this scenery for granted. Far from
being defensive of their way of life and wanting to protect it
and their land from exploitation, they are eager to cash in:

EDWARD: Apart from anything else, a Rolls Royce'll last
forever. It's a false economy to invest in cheap goods.
RODDY: It's not cheap! The Maserati's over thirty thousand.
And it's much nicer.
EDWARD: Oh I can just see you getting four or five winter
rams and a box of mackerel into the back of a Maserati.
That's what you need your Rolls for. Its adaptability.

Forsyth does not close his eyes to the fact that the townspeople are poor and have to work hard to make a living. They
all do several jobs. Roddy the barman helps on the boats.
The elderly farmers work on their land from dawn to dusk.
'Have you only got one job then?' Jonathan asks Mac envi-
ously. The villagers' willingness to sell up and Knox Oil &
Gas's determination to buy it seem to make it inevitable that
the natural beauty of the place will be destroyed forever.
But other events show us a different development, one that
opposes the deal the townspeople and Mac are trying to make.
As with the use of Mark Knopfler's sound track (see Section
5), the change in Mac is handled carefully and gradually,
built scene by scene through the narrative as other aspects
of the story unfold, and is always linked to the landscape.
Similarly, Oldsen, who has started the film as a callow and
comic version of Mac, is also changed, literally seduced by his
surroundings in the shape of the lovely Marina.

Of all the characters in the film, only Ben values the environment for what it is, and is prepared to defend it. He knows its history, understands its needs and understands exactly what Knox Oil & Gas will do to it. He knows that the beach is a fragile, complex, ever-changing ecosystem that can be affected for better or worse. It has before – as he describes to Mac and Oldsen when the three of them make their way back to his shack – and it could again. The fighter jets that scream out of the skies are not just symbols of threat; they are actually bombing the place. The bay is not permanent; it evolves constantly and is already in danger. Any slight adjustment to its water, terrain, sky or wildlife could destroy it forever. And it is Ben in the end who saves it.

We should of course respect Forsyth's words when he states that the environmental theme in *Local Hero* is deliberately light. It is obvious that this is not a film with a self-consciously profound message. It uses comedy to produce the bittersweet effect that marks all Forsyth's films, and is intended above all as a funny and poignant entertainment. But it is interesting to note that the concerns raised in the film in 1983 are still with us, as shown by Donald Trump's recent successful bid to buy a large area of Aberdeenshire coast to convert into a luxury holiday resort for wealthy tourists.[5] Opposition to these plans came from environmental groups who were concerned about the exploitation of one the world's last natural habitats, worries that were swept aside by loud assertions of increased wealth and employment in the area.

More generally, issues of the environment and sustainability are probably even more topical today than they were when *Local Hero* was made. The idea of the world's resources being finite, and the continuous consumption of them by contemporary society as being simply unaffordable, is now seen as one of the key issues in a world that has to live within its means. The culture of massive and unsustainable borrowing, be it financial or environmental, is considered by many to be no longer viable, and the threat to the environment is now global. Geddes and Watt's boastful claims in the laboratory about unfreezing the Arctic Circle may now be coming true, with disastrous consequences. Light though *Local Hero* is, it touches on deep issues that are increasingly relevant now, and it may be closer to our lives than ever before.

Displacement and loss
Hand in hand with the theme of the environment and the way it is explored goes a melancholy exploration of displacement and loss. In order to make effective comedy, Forsyth must examine sadness, and this he does through various characters in the film. The poignancy of his humour is in fact one of the key aspects of Forsyth's style.

Not all the characters in the film have homes. Mac and Happer both lack them, so intent are they on other things: in Mac's case the pursuit of money, in Happer's the need to find eternal fame. Moritz, Happer's eccentric counsellor, seems to have been hired by Happer to insult him and cause him pain. Clearly Happer has felt it necessary to do this, suggesting that he is far from happy. Mac also lives alone, although he does call a woman called Trudi, probably his ex-wife, from his bachelor apartment just before leaving Texas. The conversation ends in an argument. Mac's attitude towards Trudi seems ambivalent: he is angry with her on the phone, yet calls the rabbit he and Oldsen run down in the mist after her, and becomes upset when he accidentally eats her. Even the last vestiges of a lost relationship become an opportunity of comedy for Forsyth.

In contrast, the townspeople of Ferness live familiar and settled lives in surroundings that never change. Their way of life, their jobs and their landscape are so habitual that they take them for granted. Indeed, they are only too happy to escape from their limited existences, and rush to sell their properties to Knox Oil from the moment Mac arrives. Urquhart, when Mac and Oldsen meet him in his lawyer's office, jumps on his chair when the oilmen leave and dances a jig of delight. When the townspeople are in the church, all they want to know about is how much they will get for their homes and when they can expect it. They are not condemned for their greed, for their lives are indeed hard and constrained.

Victor, the Russian trawler man, tells Mac not to blame them
– they are poor and need to make the best of things – but
Mac begins to regret the change that will inevitably come to
the place. And Mac too is changing as his values shift and
he begins to look for different things in his life than money.
There is an ironic, and subtle, tension between the wealthy
oilmen's search for human values and a home and the local
people's willingness to give up their homes for money, that
Forsyth weaves into the drama.

Nevertheless, and despite the many humorous overtones,
there are suggestions that the townspeople will not find
happiness once they too are displaced. One local man, Peter,
mourns at the ceilidh that money has not brought him the
happiness he expected. Another serious note sounds when
the townspeople follow Ben to the beach after he has eaten
at the hotel. Their silent march is menacing. What would
they have stopped at if the arrival of the godlike Happer in
his helicopter had not interrupted them? It is a moment of
genuine threat, and one that shows the potential for violence
and human tragedy under the apparently light-hearted
search for wealth.

The incomers, however – Mac, Oldsen and Happer – all
find something in Ferness that they lack in the outside
world. Mac finds a sense of identification with the landscape,
a feeling of peace, and Stella. Oldsen finds love with Marina,
and he is steadied and calmed by her, so that by the time he
pitches the idea for a marine laboratory to Happer, he seems
like a much more mature and capable person. Happer, from
the moment he arrives, takes to the bay. All these characters
come to share with Ben a feeling of contentment they lack in
the 'real' world, a satisfaction with who they are and what
they do.

> BEN: You see, the thing is – I'm still working the place
> myself. It's my living. It supports me.
> URQUHART: You'd have lots of money. You wouldn't have
> to work.
> BEN: Oh we all have to work, Gordon. The beach has to be
> worked. Think of the state the place would get into.

Happer's talk with Ben leads him to change his plans. He will build a research institute here, not a refinery. He will spend time with Ben studying the sky through his telescope, and perhaps, with the Institute named after him, find the fame he has always wanted. He seems enthusiastic and rejuvenated, as if he has at last found a measure of happiness.

But the sense of displacement, and even loss, is strongest at the end of the film, when Mac has to return to Texas. He does not say goodbye to Stella, but looks down at her as he soars past her in the helicopter. His empty apartment in Houston, shiny with polished wood and metal, seems sterile, devoid of any human presence. He pulls shells from his pockets and sniffs them, pins pictures of himself, Gordon and Stella to his notice board, and finally pulls back the plate glass window and stands on the terrace looking out over the city as if he has lost something that can never be replaced.

The final shot of the film shows Ferness in the early morning, with the red telephone box by the pier. As we watch, the telephone starts to ring. The film ends, as ever with Forsyth, ambiguously. Will Mac ever return? And who, if anyone, will answer? The film ends with these questions left open.

In fact, Forsyth has revealed that the ending as it exists now came about because the American distributors, Warner Brothers, wanted a happier ending than he had intended. After preview screenings in Seattle, studio executives stated that they would prefer Mac not to leave forever, but to return to Ferness, to live there happily ever after. Neither Puttnam nor Forsyth were happy with this, and Puttnam challenged Forsyth to come up with an alternative ending that would satisfy the studio without compromising the film's integrity. Forsyth was unwilling to do more filming, as he had found it a huge strain. Instead, he had an idea which would preserve the ambiguity, or, as he describes it, 'a sweetness'. He remembered that there was an unused shot of the village in the early morning with the telephone box in the centre frame. This short shot allowed the audience to make up their own minds for either a happy or a sad resolution for the film. And so the famous ending came into being.

9. *LOCAL HERO*: THE ACTORS

The star: Burt Lancaster

The expression 'film star' came into being with the advent of cinema and refers particularly to that medium, and less to stage or television, because of the special role stars play in relation to the big screen.

Films need stars. These kinds of actors are different from other actors in that they work almost exclusively in films and play only lead or major roles (they do not include the many other types of actors, from character actors to extras, who also appear). Stars' names appear on the film's marketing materials and help attract the audience. Stars are powerful and frequently direct or produce films themselves. They have a great deal of influence during the making of a film and can demand changes to the script or to an aspect of the production. They are internationally famous and command huge fees. Generally, the bigger the budget for a film, the bigger and better paid the stars who appear in it.

But stars also go through different phases in their careers and make their own decisions. Although a star is often known for playing a particular kind of role, he or she will also try to avoid being typecast. So stars may seek out particular roles, accepting some and rejecting others as they try to stretch their talents without sacrificing their success.

Burt Lancaster, who plays Felix Happer in *Local Hero*, was one of Hollywood's greatest and biggest stars, with a successful film career spanning five decades. Importantly, he belonged to and was part of Hollywood's golden era, when stars were at their most powerful and influential. He came to films from the circus, where he had worked as an acrobat until injury forced him to change his occupation. He appeared at first on the big screen in a variety of roles, but always playing the leading man, known for his good looks and athleticism in playing swashbuckling roles. He was consequently dismissed by the critics. But later in his career he became known for his acting ability and his adventurousness in the roles he accepted, particularly his willingness to move away from traditional 'tough guy' roles. His many successes included *The Killers* (1947), *From Here to Eternity* (1953), *Gunfight at the O.K. Corral* (1957), *Sweet Smell of Success* (1957), *Elmer Gantry* (1960), *The Birdman of Alcatraz* (1962), *The Leopard* (1963), *The Swimmer* (1968), *Airport* (1970), *Atlantic City* (1980) and *Field of Dreams* (1989).

Lancaster also directed and produced films himself, running his own production company Hecht-Hill-Lancaster Productions. He came to have huge power, commanding enormous fees, winning an Oscar and a Golden Globe Award and hiring and firing more than one director from his productions (he sacked Sandy Mackendrick, for example, from *The Devil's Disciple*, and brought in another director) (Kemp, 49). He was widely reputed to be ruthless and demanding in his professional life. In a world which frequently avoids any political involvement for fear of unpopularity, he openly supported liberal causes and was an outspoken critic of McCarthyism and the Vietnam War. He worked with the greatest directors of his day, including Bernardo Bertolucci and Luchino Visconti. He died in 1994.

So while it might seem surprising that an actor of Lancaster's pedigree would take an interest in what might have seemed a very minor and unusual project such as *Local Hero*, his involvement was in fact very typical of his career (see Section 3). We should remember too that, although *Local Hero* was the first ever home-grown Scottish production, Lancaster would have known of earlier films with Scottish settings where magical villages and wily locals enchanted and outfoxed Americans, such as *Brigadoon* and *The Maggie*. The latter was directed by Mackendrick, who later directed Lancaster in one of his greatest films, *Sweet Smell of Success*.

Bill Forsyth, for his part, had loved Lancaster as an actor since childhood, and had written the part of Felix Happer with Lancaster in mind, although without any real hope of securing him. It is a common device when writing a screenplay to think of particular actors for the roles, as imagining them helps the writer visualise the character and 'hear' the lines. But it was only when Forsyth and Puttnam met Lancaster at the BAFTA Awards in London that Forsyth's fantasy became real. Lancaster was keen to do the film as soon as he read the script, and he was the only actor approached. To Puttnam's and Forsyth's excitement, Lancaster accepted the role. However, he demanded a huge fee which would cost the largest part of the film's budget for the cast. Puttnam and Forsyth agreed but felt sure they would be able to persuade Lancaster to accept lower wages.

They were wrong. Lancaster stuck to his guns and threatened to leave the project every time a reduction in his payment was raised. In the end, he received his full fee. But the effect of a major star's presence was electric on the rest of the cast and to everyone else involved in making the film. All the participants were suddenly aware that, having worked all their lives in a relatively small area of theatre, television or film, they were now involved in something much more significant. Peter Capaldi, in his first ever acting job, simply could not believe that he was shaking hands with Burt Lancaster. The star's presence had a similar effect on everyone else (with the exception of Forsyth's mother, who did not recognise him when they were introduced) (Forsyth, 2008). Suddenly the young actors, camera and sound people, assistants, producers and students – the budding talent of the entire Scottish film industry – realised that international fame and success were on their doorstep, and possibly achievable.

Happer and Knox: Lancaster and MacKay

Lancaster in his later years often played older men who have fallen on hard times, as in *Valdez is Coming* and *Atlantic City*. Despite his wealth and divine power, Felix Happer is cast from this mould. There is something needy about his quest for fame and his wish to have a comet or an institute or anything long lasting named after him. We see him alone at home. We witness him hunted from his office, pursued from the building he owns like a fugitive. He is not married and has no children, and Lancaster brings out his feelings of regret and unhappiness.

But there is an important moment in the film where Happer's predicament is resolved, and it is the turning point of the film. When Happer arrives in Ferness to take over the negotiation from Mac, he is confident he can persuade Ben to sell the beach, even asking Mac if he has offered the beachcomber a piano. But he also is intrigued to hear that Ben's second name is Knox. Ben's link to the past and to what he owns is authentic, unlike Happer's. There are documents in a museum in Edinburgh to prove it.

We do not see on screen what happens between the two older men when they meet. Happer enters the beachcomber's makeshift home through its front window, and Mac and Urquhart are dismissed. While the younger men and the rest of the villagers wait anxiously, the two older men can be heard laughing uproariously. It is the first time in the film when Happer has been shown to be joyful and free from care. And when he does eventually emerge, it is with a different plan, one that resolves the whole conflict. The bay will be turned into a marine institute and observatory; the beach will be saved; the local people will be paid and keep their jobs; Happer will have something permanent to leave behind; and Marina and Oldsen will help run the new institution and will live (and swim) together happily ever after. Only Mac, condemned to return to his lonely life in Houston, is the loser.

Like all the scenes in *Local Hero*, the drama is understated and subtle, but it is clear that Happer and Ben are similar to each other, each one the mirror of the other. Both are towards the ends of their long lives. Both have spent those lives in pursuit of ideals. Happer has sought the stars, the ephemeral glory of the planets, looking always upwards. Ben has cared for the ground, the solid nature of the soil and sand, its past and its future, looking always down. Happer is wealthy and successful but unhappy. Ben lives on other people's cast-offs, the fruit he finds on the shore or the sandwiches he fills his pockets with at the ceilidh; he has almost nothing, not even a proper house to live in. In most people's eyes he is little more than a vagrant; and yet he is satisfied and fulfilled. He has what Happer lacks, as his real link with the land he lives on proves. Ben is also ready to stand up and fight for what he believes in, while Happer is surrounded by yes-men so fearful of him that they fail to wake him during a meeting. Ben loves the beach and his way of life: he is prepared to risk everything for it. There is no love in Happer's life, either for another person or for what he does. He has little interest in his company, caring nothing about the negotiation or the land about to be bought, obsessed only with the heavens and what is beyond his reach. Even his own psychologist stalks him, the most insulting thing about the situation being that Happer is paying him to do it. The millionaire's life is hollow; the beachcomber's is full and rich.

But when the two men meet this changes. The fact that this important moment happens off-screen makes it even more comic and poignant. For the first time in the film we hear Happer laugh out loud. The meeting is not businesslike – it is social. They send Oldsen for roast beef sandwiches and whisky. What has seemed of life-changing importance to the villagers is shown to be only of passing interest to the older men. What they are concentrating on is their enjoyment of their talk and their shared interests. (Ben owns a telescope, and knows as much as Happer about the skies around this part of the world.) It is clear, when Happer finally leaves Ben and starts to tell Mac how his plans have changed, that the two men have struck up a friendship. For the first time we see Happer happy, full of enthusiasm for his plans, brimming with new ideas, as if he is young again. As he strides off towards the sea in the last shot in which he appears, he walks with the bounce and optimism of a man with much to look forward to, in contrast to his slumped, apathetic, bored demeanour earlier. It is also clear that Ben, not Happer, has been the one who struck the deal. The arch-negotiator has been out-negotiated, and the canny local, apparently much less worldly wise, has fooled the supposedly more sophisticated traveller.

As well as working inside the film, this scene also operates outside it and within the context of the film industry. In the first place, it deliberately refers to other films such as *The Maggie* and *Brigadoon*, where locals deceive and mislead seemingly more sophisticated visitors. It is an example of *intertextuality*, or deliberate referencing to other films, as discussed earlier (see Section 3). In the second place, it is a dramatic trope, or commonly seen device, to have the whole of a conflict depend on two apparently opposed camps – warring families or powerful men – who, when they finally come together, find they have no real conflict. The ironic outcome is that much of the rest of the story, and the efforts of the other characters who have been engaged in the fight until that point, are shown to have been unnecessary. As Mac and Gordon pour themselves one last whisky in the hotel before Mac's departure, they reflect ruefully that it has all been for nothing. Mac has changed, fallen in love, seen the stars and altered his whole way of looking at the world, but it has made no difference – he must return to his old way of life. (Mac's situation when he arrives back in Houston, in fact, echoes that of Happer's at the start of the film, as if Happer has handed him his burden of unhappiness. Alone in his apartment, he slides back a dividing screen and stares out at lights just as Happer once did in his penthouse, as if what he truly desires lies forever beyond his reach.)

But in the third place – and most importantly – the institution of film helps tell the story and assists the poignancy and meaning of the scene because of the two actors involved. Both Lancaster and MacKay were veterans of their respective acting cultures; both were men of great achievement in different ways. MacKay was one of Scotland's most respected and experienced actors, instilling in many of the parts he played a sense of rock-like endurance and stubborn tenacity. Whether playing the unsympathetic character of Mr McKay the prison warder in *Porridge*, or a more sympathetic one like Ben in *Local Hero*, he invested all the roles he played with a sense of unflinching strength, an ability to endure and withstand any force. He was a worthy opponent for Lancaster, an actor known for his relentless drive and intimidating physical presence. Indeed, Fulton MacKay was one of the few performers in Scotland capable of holding his own against a star like Lancaster, and he does so throughout the film, offering within the narrative a convincingly grounded counterweight to Happer's heavenly aspirations.

In a similar way, again outside the film and therefore part of the industry rather than the narrative, MacKay and

Lancaster represented two sides of the theatrical world that rarely met, the Scottish and the Hollywood ones. On the one hand, a hugely successful and internationally renowned film star, part of the best-known film tradition in the world; on the other, a highly respected but local actor, little known outside the UK, whose career was spent in television and the stage because of the lack of an indigenous film industry. In acting terms, despite Lancaster's much greater fame, there is nothing to choose between the two men. In terms of achievement within their different traditions, both rose to the very top of their professions. And yet Fulton MacKay remained virtually unknown. It is interesting to reflect whether the scene between the two characters resembled the situation between the two men, one famous, the other home grown, but with a sense of equality and mutual respect, and perhaps even friendship, between them. Whether Forsyth intended it in his casting or not, the choice of Lancaster and MacKay in the roles of Happer and Ben illustrates the similarities and differences between the Scottish and American film industries.

The other actors:
Peter Riegert (MacInyre)
Peter Riegert went on to a distinguished career in American film and television, including appearances in *The Sopranos* (2001–6), *The Mask* (1994) and *Traffic* (2000), which won him the Screen Actors' Guild Award. He has also directed films.

Denis Lawson (Gordon Urquhart)
Denis Lawson has appeared in a wide range of roles on stage and screen, including the original *Star Wars* trilogy (1980), where he played ace pilot Wedge Antilles, *Bleak House* (2005), *Hornblower* (1998) and *Robin Hood* (2007).

Peter Capaldi (Danny Oldsen)
Peter Capaldi went on after *Local Hero* to appear in many other films and TV series, including Ken Russell's *The Lair of the White Worm* (1988), *Minder* (1985), *Skins* (2007–9), *Waking the Dead* (2007), *Peep Show* (2004) and *Dr Who*

(2008). His best-known television role is as Malcolm Tucker in the political satire *The Thick of It* (2005–9), which in 2009 transferred to the big screen as *In the Loop*. He also won an Oscar and a BAFTA in 1995 for directing the short film *Franz Kafka's It's a Wonderful Life*.

Jenny Seagrove (Marina)

Jenny Seagrove is an English actress whose stage credits include *Jane Eyre, Present Laughter* and *Brief Encounter*. She has appeared on television in dramas such as *Diana* (1984), *A Woman of Substance* (1984) and *Judge John Deed* (2001–7), and in films such as *Appointment with Death* (1988) and *The Guardian* (1990). *Local Hero* was her first major film role.

Jennifer Black (Stella)

Jennifer Black has appeared in many other screen dramas including *Rebus* (2006–7), *River City* (2007), *The Bill* (1994) and *Taggart* (1996, 2002).

Rikki Fulton (Geddes)

Rikki Fulton was one of Scotland's best-known comic actors, famous for his double-act with Jack Milroy in the 1960s as *Francie and Josie*, two Glaswegian teddy boys, and for his long-running TV series *Scotch and Wry* (1987–92), a sketch show where he appeared as several long-running characters, including the Reverend I. M. Jolly. He was also a straight actor, with appearances in the 1982 film *Gorky Park* as a vicious KGB officer and in *Comfort and Joy* (1984), Forsyth's follow-up movie to *Local Hero*. He made guest appearances in *Rab C. Nesbitt* and played the role of Dan Macphail in the BBC version of *The Tales of Para Handy* with Gregor Fisher (1994–95). He died in 2004.

Alex Norton (Norman Watt)

Alex Norton is best-known today for his role as DCI Burke in *Taggart* (2002–2010), but in his long career he has also played parts in *Dr Finlay's Casebook* (1965–70), *Gregory's Girl* (1981), Bill Douglas's epic film *Comrades* (1986), *Little Voice* (1998), *Orphans* (1997), *Patriot Games* (1992),

Braveheart (1995) and *Pirates of the Caribbean: Dead Man's Chest* (2006). He was one of the founder members of the 7:84 company, touring Scotland with *The Cheviot, the Stag and the Black, Black Oil.* He also directed the first stage production of Tony Roper's *The Steamie.*

Fulton MacKay (Ben Knox)

Fulton MacKay was one of Scotland's leading actors. Most of his work was on the stage, with appearances in *The Naked Island, The Lower Depths, Peer Gynt, The Alchemist* and *Nicholas Nickleby.* Apart from *Local Hero,* he appeared in only a few movies, including *Gumshoe* (1971), *Britannia Hospital* (1982) and *Defence of the Realm* (1985). His most famous screen role was on television, as Mr McKay, the ferocious prison warder, in *Porridge* (1974–77) with Ronnie Barker. He also played the original lighthouse keeper in the children's series *Fraggle Rock* (1983–87). He wrote plays for the BBC under the pseudonym of Aeneas MacBride. He died in 1987.

Norman Chancer (Moritz)

Norman Chancer is an American actor who has appeared in other film and television roles in *Reds* (1981), *Victor Victoria* (1982) and *Kavanagh QC* (1997). He also provides the voiceover for the TV animated character *Sonic the Hedgehog* (1993–95).

Christopher Asante (Reverend Murdo MacPherson)

Christopher Asante was a Ghanaian actor who appeared in British television series in the 1980s and 90s, including *Space: 1999* (1977), *Hazell* (1979), *The Professionals* (1980) and *Desmond's* (1989–94). He returned to Ghana in 1995 where he became a Cultural Ambassador. He died in 2000.

Christopher Rozycki (Victor)

Christopher Rozycki is a Polish-born actor who has appeared in many British-made series and films, including *Bergerac* (1981), *Truly, Madly, Deeply* (1990), *A Perfect Spy* (1986) and *Sleepers* (1991).

Tam Dean Burn (Roddy)

Tam Dean Burn is a Scottish actor who has gone on to appear in many stage and television roles, including *Taggart* (1992), Irvine Welsh's *The Acid House* (1998), *Young Adam* (2003), *Holby City* (2007) and *One Night in Emergency* (2010).

Charles Kearney (Peter)

Charles Kearney is a Scottish character actor who has appeared in many Scottish film and television productions, including the original *The View from Daniel Pike* (1971), *The Wicker Man* (1972), *Sutherland's Law* (1973), *Comfort and Joy* (1984), *Taggart* (1986), *Rab C. Nesbitt* (1992) and *Breaking the Waves* (1996).

James Kennedy (Edward)

James Kennedy was a well-known stage and screen character actor whose credits included *Sutherland's Law* (1973), *Huntingtower* (1976), *The Camerons* (1979), *The White Bird Passes* (1980), *Mackenzie* (1980) and *Crusoe* (1988).

Karen Douglas (Mrs Wyatt)

Karen Douglas has recently appeared in short films such as *Breakfast* (2002) and the children's DVD *Morticia* directed by Nabil Shaban (2008).

Jimmy Yuill (Iain)

Jimmy Yuill has had a long career mostly in the theatre, although he has also acted in films directed by Kenneth Branagh, including *Much Ado About Nothing* (1993) and *As You Like It* (2006). He is a member of the Royal Shakespeare Company.

John Gordon Sinclair (Ricky)

John Gordon Sinclair is the village's young tearaway, Ricky, who also plays drums in the Ace Tones, the band that plays at the ceilidh. He had been cast as the lead in Forsyth's previous film *Gregory's Girl*, a comic film of adolescent love set in Cumbernauld, and it is as Gregory that he will always be remembered. But he has continued to have a successful

career on stage, film, radio and television, appearing in
the television series *Hot Metal* (1986), John Byrne's *Your
Cheatin' Heart* (1990), radio adaptations of Iain Banks's
Espedair Street (1998) and A. J. Cronin's *Adventures of a
Black Bag* (2001–2), a live performance of Mike Oldfield's
Tubular Bells II staged at Edinburgh castle (1992) and, not
least, as Gregory again in *Gregory's 2 Girls* (1999), Forsyth's
film about the same character twenty years later. He also
took over as the lighthouse keeper in *Fraggle Rock* in 1987.

Kenny Ireland (Skipper)
Kenny Ireland is a leading theatre director whose credits
include *Guys and Dolls, A View from the Bridge, Romeo and
Juliet, Waiting for Godot* and *A Midsummer Night's Dream.*
He has also appeared in the television series *Benidorm*
(2007–9) and *Taggart* (1988), and the feature film *The Big
Man* with Liam Neeson (1990).

David Mowat (Gideon)
David Mowat was a veteran Scottish actor who appeared
in *Dr Finlay's Casebook* (1970), *Sutherland's Law* (1973),
Armchair Theatre (1971) and *Play for Today* (1979).

Willy Joss (Sandy)
Willy Joss was also one of Scotland's leading veteran actors,
with appearances in films and television stretching back to
the 1960s, including *Ring of Bright Water* (1969), *The Duna
Bull* (1972) and *The Eagle of the Ninth* (1976). *Local Hero*
was his last screen appearance.

Jonathan Watson (Jonathan)
Jonathan Watson is a Scottish comedian and impressionist
best known for his satirical television programme *Only an
Excuse* (1996–2003). He has also appeared in straight and
comic roles in *City Lights* (1984–1991), *Casualty* (2001) and
The Bill (2007).

Caroline Guthrie (Pauline)
Caroline Guthrie, who plays the punk girl who pursues

Oldsen at the ceilidh, also appeared in Forsyth's other films, *Gregory's Girl* and *Comfort and Joy* (1982), and has since gone on to roles in *Chaplin* (1989), *Glasgow Kiss* (2001) and *Casualty* (2007).

Dave Anderson (Fraser)

Dave Anderson has worked as an actor, musician and musical director for numerous Scottish theatres companies including 7:84 and Wildcat. His other film credits include *Gregory's Girl* (1981), *Heavenly Pursuits* (1985), *Orphans* (1997) and *Post Mortem* (1998). On television he is best known for his appearances in the long running BBC sitcom *City Lights*. He has also played roles in *The Avengers* (1964), *Taggart* (1986), *Tutti Frutti* (1987), *Rab C. Nesbitt* (1990, 1998), *Monarch of the Glen* (2003), *Still Game* (2007) and many other shows.

Ida Shuster (woman at ceilidh)

Ida Shuster is a veteran Scottish actress with stage and screen appearances dating from the 1960s, including *Dr Finlay's Casebook* (1963–70), *Death Watch* (1980), *Hamish MacBeth* (1996), *Still Game* (2002–04) and *Taggart* (1990–2005). In 2008, at the age of ninety, she became the first woman to lay a wreath at the Association of Jewish Ex-Servicemen's Remembrance parade.

Other Production Team members:
Iain Brown (NFS student attachment)

Iain Brown, a young student at the National Film School in the early 1980s, was attached to the film on placement during the shooting of *Local Hero*.

Iain Smith (Associate Producer)

Iain Smith has since gone on to be a successful international film producer, with *The Killing Fields* (1984), *City of Joy* (1992), *Seven Years in Tibet* (1997), *Alexander* (2004) and *The A-Team* (2010) among his many credits. His feature film *The Bonny Boys* is in production at the time of writing.

10. CRITICAL RECEPTION AND THE FILM'S LEGACY

Local Hero was released in February 1983, first in the USA and then in the UK and other territories. There were no advance festival screenings but, nevertheless, it was launched with a real sense of anticipation. There had been an extraordinary level of interest throughout the production period with documentary film crews from Scottish Television and others, including one of the authors of this booklet, behind the scenes following every step of the process (Scott, A., 1983). Many journalists had visited the locations in Houston and Scotland, and this close attention led to high hopes for the film before any audience had paid to see it. At the same time as the film was to be launched the script had been adapted into a novel by David Benedictus, published by Penguin. *Local Hero* was in the press, in the bookshops and now in the cinemas.

Many commentators looked to this film to find out how its producer David Puttnam's work would develop after winning the Academy Award for Best Film with his previous project. Also, British (and particularly Scottish) critics wondered how Bill Forsyth's career would develop and whether he could succeed as a writer/director with a fully funded project and an international cast of professional actors, so unlike his previous hits which had fallen into the low-budget category.

The first response from US film critics was warm and supportive. They were charmed by Forsyth's modern fable and intrigued by his idiosyncratic approach:

> Genuine fairy stories are rare; so is film-making that is thoroughly original in an unobtrusive way. Forsyth's quirky disarming film is both, and it's also proof that *Gregory's Girl* was more than a happy accident. *Local Hero* demonstrates Forsyth's uncanny ability for making an audience sense something that isn't easily explained. (Maslin, *New York Times*)

> Here is a small film to treasure, a loving, funny, understated portrait of a small Scottish town ... What could have been a standard plot about conglomerates and ecology etc.,

turns into a wicked study of human nature ... What makes
the material really work is the low-key approach of Forsyth
and his patience to let his characters gradually reveal themselves to the camera ... Nothing is more absorbing than
human personalities, developed with love and humour.
Some of the pay-offs in this film are sly and subtle, and
others generate big laughs. (Ebert, *Chicago Sun-Times*)

This positive reaction by leading columnists was further
nurtured by a marketing campaign in the USA which tried
to present the film as a 'high-concept' idea and which drew
attention to the mystical undertones of the story, focusing
almost exclusively on the two American actors, Lancaster and
Reigert. The high-concept approach to selling a film presup-
poses that a central concept and image should run through
all aspects of the film, including the marketing campaign,
the trailer, the posters and the merchandising produced to
promote the film.

But it proved difficult to summarise Forsyth's subtle script
in this way. In an interview during filming, Puttnam reflected
that he was always surprised at the negative responses he
had had from potential investors during pre-production,
despite the fact that every response from the creative talents
(including Lancaster) had been positive. Forsyth's script
didn't fit any easy category, perhaps because its understated
nuances, ironic humour and lightness of touch were at odds
with the high-concept ideal, and needed to be carefully
explored rather than summarised in a neat (and misleading)
précis. But the distributors still followed the high-concept
strategy. They used images on the poster that emphasised
the big-name star and brought out the themes of the film in
very simple ways. Lancaster and Riegert were shown in suits
but barefoot, paddling in the sea, as seagulls circle overhead
and mountains are shown in distance. The North American
trailer for the film emphasised Highland stereotypes, a
narrator drawling over images taken from the film:

There is a place where the Northern Lights transform the
sky ... Modern mermaids spring from the sea ... The land

breathes with an ancient mystery ... And all who witness
its wonders come to believe in its magic ... *Local Hero* ...
the story of an ordinary man who cared enough to do something extraordinary ... (Meir, 191)

Despite the fact that the marketing style did not really
reflect the film, audiences in the USA, like the critics, found
the story appealing and amusing and it was widely supported,
even if it revealed the hollow reality of life in an expensive
Houston high-rise apartment.

British audiences also liked the film and it performed well
at the box-office. Here the critics again concentrated on what
they perceived as gentle, observational humour. The Scottish
attitude towards *Local Hero* by the press, however, was less
favourable, implying that it was a film which missed its target
through the 'allegedly frivolous pursuit of benign comedic
irony' (Murray, 2005, 219). This denigration of *Local Hero*,
viewing it as some kind of innocent whimsical ephemera,
missed the point of Forsyth's lasting vision, which was much
more complex and with darker undertones (Murray, 2011).
There is no doubt that expectations had also been raised
because the film represented a potential great leap forward
for the film industry in this small country. Perhaps they had
been raised too high. It seemed impossible to judge *Local
Hero* on its own terms, or to appreciate and understand its
quality as a movie. It was as though critics were awaiting the
creation of a new national cinema. Writing a few years later
Forsyth's old partner, Charlie Gormley, reflected that no one
really knew what was meant by a Scottish film:

> Sure as hell, if the local critical backbiting is to be believed,
> it wouldn't be a Bill Forsyth film. Bill, it seems, has gone
> from winning the game for Scotland to vaguely letting the
> side down. (Gormley, 190)

In some ways the initial negative critical reaction was
an accident of timing because of contemporary debates and
academic theories. In 1981, whilst Forsyth was writing the
script for *Local Hero*, another Scottish film maker, Murray

Grigor (together with his wife Barbara), devised and curated a large-scale exhibition entitled *Scotch Myths*, which investigated and – in its own view – exposed 'shortbread tin' tartan kitsch which celebrated a phoney sense of Scottish history, dating, it has often been claimed, from the romantic stories of Sir Walter Scott and his invention of the myth of the Highlands at the time of George IVs visit to Scotland in 1822. The exhibition struck a chord with other cultural commentators and led to a conference entitled *Scotch Reels* as part of the Edinburgh International Film Festival in August 1982. Grigor was also commissioned to produce a feature length film for the new Channel 4 which would be screened on New Year's Eve 1982. At the *Scotch Reels* event delegates watched classic Scottish films such as *The Gorbals Story* (MacKane, 1950) and *Brigadoon* and debated what attributes and qualities they would like to see in a vigorous, modern film and television industry in Scotland. There was much discussion about the possible impact of both *Local Hero*, still in the cutting room, and also the film policy of Channel 4 which was attracting the attention of many Scottish directors. In the *Scotch Reels* collection of essays (McArthur, 1980) produced following the conference, Colin McArthur, John Caughie and others bemoaned the paucity and poverty of Scottish images on screen and identified three dominant genres of Scottish film narrative, all of them, in their view, misleading and unrepresentative. First, there was 'Tartanry', a direct descendant of the novels of Sir Walter Scott and his romanticisation of the Highlands, the Scottish clan system and the Jacobite uprisings. Then there was 'Kailyard', derived from the rural novels of J.M. Barrie and other supposedly sentimental authors, a tradition of whimsical comedies in which life in the countryside and small towns of the Lowlands was presented as a simple ideal. Finally, there was 'Clydesidism', in which the urban working-class culture of the large Victorian industrial cities (especially Glasgow) was presented as the true representation of Scottish identity.

As the foundational text of Scottish film and television studies, the influence of *Scotch Reels* was enormous. As a work of criticism it has since been greatly scrutinised. Taking a broadly Marxist view, it excluded some filmmakers who certainly deserved to be in it (such as Bill Douglas), and called for a radical realism within Scottish film to the exclusion of all other approaches. In the essays presented at the conference, these critics called for a new kind of Scottish filmmaking which would turn its back on Tartanry and the legacy of *Brigadoon*, leave behind the stereotypical Scottish caricatures of the Kailyard reproduced in the comedies of the Ealing Studios, and even disregard Clydesidism and the working class images of the industrial city. They called for a new Scottish cinema. But, in the same way that radically avant-garde representations of Scotland could be overlooked for being too unfamiliar (Neely, 3), when the new Scottish cinema did arrive in the form of *Local Hero*, which used the familiar in new ways, the academic and critical worlds represented by the *Scotch Reels* authors simply failed to recognise it.

With *That Sinking Feeling* the Scottish press had promoted the idea of the hidden gem, of a plucky no-budget underdog. They had adored a guileless non-professional teenage comedy with local accents and local jokes of *Gregory's Girl*. Now, although the new film had been launched with great publicity and hype in Scotland (its opening night was in Glasgow), newspaper reviewers did not welcome it with the acclaim they had lavished on Forsyth's previous releases. Perhaps there was a sense of *schadenfreude*, the feeling that the writer/director might have over-reached himself, overstepped the mark with his new film. To many, *Local Hero* seemed to lack the satirical cutting edge of Forsyth's other work, and to be too stereotypical a portrayal of Scotland, similar in many ways to Hollywood versions of Scotland such as *Brigadoon*. Indeed, the magical and mythical way in which the village was portrayed in the film reminded many critics of traditional Scottish representations they would rather forget, couthy rural images in line with forgotten British quirky comedies, and, even worse, the much-maligned 'Kailyard' movement (Sillars, 123). In addition, the film's producer, David Puttnam, had negotiated tie-in promotions with the Scottish Tourist Board and John Menzies Outfitters, and had arranged screenings for schools under the banner of showing schoolchildren what the Highlands were like (Meir, 192). Generally, the marketing for the film played precisely towards what many critics were saying about the film itself: that it showed an outdated and misleading version of Scotland which had been shown many times before. In other words, this most un-Hollywood-like of films was accused of having sold out to Hollywood.

But despite these first and continuing reactions *Local Hero* did relatively well at the box office, finding a longer life in the cinemas than is the case with most films. While major releases tend to depend on their first weeks to take in their return of investment and profits, *Local Hero*, first released in some cities on 17 February 1983, with a later launch in others, was still playing in some areas by 11 July, indicating that audiences were watching it in different ways from Hollywood blockbusters (Meir, 194). Indeed, as time went on the main means by which *Local Hero* was promoted increasingly resembled the way major art house films are distributed, relying much more on gradual release, word of mouth publicity and extended cinema runs than the short profitable burst of the Hollywood blockbuster. The eventual success of the film and the means by which it was achieved indicates that the film's promoters and producers probably came to understand *Local Hero's* real value better than they had when it was first marketed, and over the longer term managed to get it to the audience that appreciated and liked it. According to Forsyth himself, the film did exactly as a small British production was expected to at the box office, which is to say modestly. It was not until ten or fifteen years after the film was released that he began to receive royalty payments, a testament to the film's longevity rather than its short-term impact (Forsyth, 2008).

It is possible to chart how the critical response to Forsyth has developed and shifted over the past three decades. Reviewing *Local Hero* in *Sight and Sound*, Spring 1983, Nick Roddick wrote:

> While *Whisky Galore* could still make contact with a genuine sense of traditional community, *Local Hero* can only do so self-consciously ... (Roddick, 138)

Later that year Scottish screenwriter John Brown inter-
viewed Forsyth for the next issue of *Sight and Sound* and he
replied to the criticism:

Well I'm not complaining but I do feel misunderstood ...
the films I've made have always had a much darker side
to them and it makes me wonder if there really is much
understanding of what irony is. (Brown, 204)

Meanwhile, throughout that year, Forsyth was busy at
work countering the critics with another different type of
movie. He wrote a new, contemporary comedy, starring Bill
Paterson, set against the backdrop of the notorious ice-cream
wars of the Glasgow drug gangs. Filming of *Comfort and Joy*
(1984) was completed just before Christmas 1983. After this
he worked in America on *Housekeeping* (1987), *Breaking In*
(1989) and *Being Human* (1993). He did not return to make
a 'Scottish' film again until 1999 when he wrote and directed
Gregory's 2 Girls which revisited the main character from
Gregory's Girl twenty years later.

In 1990, in a new collection of essays examining film and
television in Scotland, *From Limelight to Satellite,* Forsyth
was again charged with being charming and whimsical but
the darker universal themes of 'loss, loneliness and isola-
tion' (Hunter, 156) in his work were now acknowledged. In
Scotland in Film (1990), Forsyth Hardy acknowledged the
importance of 'two Bills' – Forsyth and Douglas – in bringing
films from Scotland to an international audience in the 1980s.
However, during the 1990s and noughties *Local Hero* mostly
dropped off the critical radar, although there were exceptions
(Bruce, 200–5). Most interest was directed towards the impact
of more recent movies such as *Shallow Grave* (Boyle, 1994)
and *Trainspotting* (Boyle, 1996), while any residual interest
in *Local Hero* focused on an examination of the importance
of its geography and locations and its lasting appeal with
the Scottish Tourist Board. The haunting sense of place in
the film was what lingered, the public fascination with the
areas associated with the film persisting in a British survey
of favourite film locations. Indeed, the use of the village of

Pennan as the fictional Ferness in *Local Hero* topped the poll in a public vote taken by the Film Distributors' Association and VisitBritain in November 2005 (Jury).

However, Forsyth's films in general, and *Local Hero* in particular, still tended to be regarded as light, ineffective and trite (Petrie, 156). It was the film's fate to be dismissed by the academic critical establishment (Meir, 190), or not acknowledged at all (Petrie, 209). This long-term critical reaction in Scotland probably contributed to the rapidity with which *Local Hero* was overlooked and even forgotten (Murray, 2010). Although an important event in its day, few would claim that a Scottish film industry had been established or inspired as a result of it, or that there had been any sort of a breakthrough in cultural terms. But in fact all these things did happen with and through *Local Hero*, as has become clear more recently. The fact that a Scottish film maker could make a big budget film in Scotland, attracting American investment and a major Hollywood star; the fact that a Scottish film maker could make a chain of successful films and then beat a path to Hollywood (Forsyth and Puttnam were both to cross the Atlantic a few years later); the fact that a Scottish story and Scottish themes could be shown on screen and interpreted enjoyably by international audiences; in short, the fact that it was possible to make a relatively big film in Scotland, inspired a new generation of young Scottish film and television makers (Scott, 206–221), many of whom were involved in the making of *Local Hero*.

Today the true impact of *Local Hero* is widely acknowledged. Whether training to be a director, a producer, a writer, an actor or any other member of the film production team, young hopefuls in Scotland were entranced by Forsyth's trailblazing success, and by his films. Less rigid than the marketing experts, and much more fluid and open to new ideas than the ideological viewpoints of the academic theorists, young filmmakers saw little to criticise in Forsyth's film and much to emulate in the way he had gone about building his career in a way that was supposed not to be possible in Scotland. Forsyth's determination to make films in exactly his own way, ignoring both the film industry's and the critics' views on how and why things were meant to happen in the way they did, showed young up-and-coming film makers the necessary amount of independent action and mental toughness. The legacy of *Local Hero*, therefore, sprang not so much from the film's content than from what Forsyth's example meant to others.

Ten years after *Local Hero*, another Scottish film, a noir thriller called *Shallow Grave*, broke through the same barrier as its precursor and achieved major international success, but this time film makers, critics and audiences in Scotland and outside it were ready for it. Its follow-up by the same producing/directing team, *Trainspotting*, achieved levels of interest and profit that no Scottish film had received before, and attracted overseas funding for subsequent Hollywood-inspired epics such as *Braveheart* and *Rob Roy*. Today, although the Scottish film industry has suffered setbacks as well as triumphs, it does exist, and may be on the verge of being able to define itself as a national cinema (Martin-Jones, 214–230). Bill Forsyth's films, and especially *Local Hero*, constitute one of the most important early moments of that development. It is true to say that without *Local Hero* the Scottish film industry could not have developed as it did.

Forsyth's achievement was finally acknowledged on the 25th anniversary of the release of the film. In February 2008, members of the cast and crew gathered at the Glasgow Film Festival for a special sell-out screening. Later in the year film critic Mark Kermode and the BBC *Culture Show* persuaded Forsyth to return to Pennan, and the *Local Hero* village location, for an item in which he talked for the first time in more than twenty years about the making of the film and watched the movie together with a local audience as he, and they, celebrated its lasting resonances (Kermode, 2008). The 2009 BAFTA Scotland Lifetime Achievement Award finally recognised Forsyth's real achievement, and honoured the crucial importance of his films to the Scottish film industry. Forsyth had shown that it was possible to make movies in a small country.

Most recently, in April 2010, The New York Film Forum screened a season of Forsyth films and the film's international appeal was recognised. That international success has been very important in terms of how Scotland has been portrayed to cinema audiences throughout the UK, in the United States and throughout the world. It is also evidence of the film's lasting appeal. The constant stream of visitors to Pennan, the affectionate tributes to the film on various websites, and the film's continuing impact on audiences are telling measures of its enduring charm and longevity. Perhaps over time the film did exert a kind of magic, becoming an enduring success in an industry known for its ephemeral nature, in its own way a classic, taking its rightful place alongside *Whisky Galore!*, *Brigadoon* and *The Maggie*. It continues to be popular in cinemas, on DVD and on television – especially in the USA – today.

NOTES

1. This technical term refers to the gauge, or width, of film used in film-making, which in turn affects the rest of the equipment. Sixteen millimetre, originally introduced in the 1920s as a cheaper alternative to thirty-two millimetre film (which is usually preferred in the making of feature films), became increasingly popular for use in documentary films and, when it was introduced, television. It was replaced in the 1980s by video.

2. But this story is partly apocryphal. According to other reports the sticking point was money, filming being less expensive in the States than on location. Gene Kelly was angry that the film was not to be made in Scotland, and Alan Jay Lerner, who helped write the music, felt that the cast should have been Scottish (Hardy, 2).

3. When a film is being made, it is important to check the 'rushes' (unedited sections of film shot day by day) on a big screen for focus, clarity and so on, as a small screen will not necessarily show every flaw.

4. One documentary, *Getting In On The Action*, was screened at the *Scotch Reels* event at the Edinburgh International Film Festival in 1982, and won the award for Best Documentary at the Celtic Film & Television Festival, Glasgow, March 1983.

5. In October 2010, Robert Gordon's University awarded Donald Trump an honorary doctorate in recognition of his 'business acumen and vision for the north-east'.

BIBLIOGRAPHY

Brown, J., 'A Suitable Job for a Scot: An Interview with Bill Forsyth', *Sight and Sound*, Summer 1983

Bruce, D., *Scotland the Movie*, Edinburgh: Polygon, 1996

Ebert, R., *Chicago Sun-Times* 15 April 1983

Edensor, T., *National Identity, Popular Culture and Everyday Life*, Oxford: Berg, 2002

Gormley, C., 'The Impact of Channel 4', *From Limelight to Satellite: A Scottish Film Book*, Dick, E. (ed.), London: BFI, 1990

Hardy, F., *Scotland in Film*, Edinburgh: EUP, 1990

Hunter, A., 'Bill Forsyth: The Imperfect Anarchist', *From Limelight to Satellite; A Scottish Film Book*, Dick, E. (ed.), London: BFI, 1990

Hunter, A., 'Being Human: Interview with Bill Forsyth', *Sight and Sound*, Vol. 4 No 8 p.27, 1994

Jury, L., 'Location, Location, Location: A Movie Buff's Choice', *The Independent*, 23 July 2005

Kemp, P., 'Mackendrickland', *Sight and Sound*, 58:1, pp. 48–52, London: BFI, Winter 1988

McArthur, C. (ed.), *Scotch Reels*, London: BFI, 1982

MacNab, G., 'Burt Lancaster: The Last Real Action Hero', 25 February 2008

Manderson, D., *Scotnote: Rob Roy by Michael Caton-Jones*, Glasgow: ASLS, 2009

Martin-Jones, D., *Global Cinema: Genres, Modes and Identities*, Edinburgh: EUP, 2009

Maslin, J., 'Film Review: Houston to Scotland Odyssey', *New York Times*, 17 February 1983

Meir, C., 'Chasing Crossover: Selling Scottish Cinema Abroad', *Scottish Cinema Now*, Murray, J., Farley, F., and Stoneman, R. (eds.), pp. 188–205, Newcastle: Cambridge Scholars, 2009

Murray, J., 'Kids in America: Narratives of Transatlantic Influence in 1990s Scottish Cinema', *Screen*, Vol. 46, Issue 2, pp. 217–226, Oxford: OUP, 2005

Murray, J., *Discomfort and Joy: The Cinema of Bill Forsyth*, Oxford: Peter Lang, 2011

Neely, S. and Riach, A., 'Demons in the Machine: Experimental Film, Poetry and Modernism in Twentieth-Century Scotland', *Scottish Cinema Now*, Murray, J., Farley, F., and Stoneman, R. (eds.), pp. 1–19, Newcastle: Cambridge Scholars, 2009

Perrone, P., 'Gerry Rafferty: Obituary', *The Independent*, 6 January 2011

Petrie, D., *Screening Scotland*, London: BFI, 2000

Petrie, D., *Contemporary Scottish Fictions: Film, Television and the Novel*, Edinburgh: EUP, 2004

Roddick, N., 'A Light in the Sky', *Sight and Sound*, Vol. 52, No 2, 1983

Sarris, A., 'Local Hero', *Village Voice*, February 22, 1983

Sillars, J., 'Admitting the Kailyard', *Scottish Cinema Now*, Murray, J., Farley, F., and Stoneman, R. (eds.), pp. 206–221, Newcastle: Cambridge Scholars, 2009

Scott, A., 'What's the Point of Film School, or, What did Beaconsfield Studios Ever do for the Scottish Film Industry?', *Scottish Cinema Now*, Murray, J., Farley, F., and Stoneman, R. (eds.), pp. 206–221, Newcastle: Cambridge Scholars, 2009

Sherington, J., *"To Speak its Pride": Films of Scotland: The Work of the Films of Scotland committee 1938–1982*, Glasgow: Scottish Film Council, 1996

SELECT FILMOGRAPHY

Boyle, D., *Shallow Grave*, Film4, 1994

Boyle, D., *Trainspotting*, PolyGram, 1996

Caton-Jones, M., *Rob Roy*, United Artists, 1995

Donlon, H., *Bill Forsyth Interview at the 2009 Ibiza Film Festival*, Kuschty Rye Production

Douglas, B., *My Childhood*, BFI, 1972

Forsyth, B., *Gregory's Girl*, Scottish Television, 1981

Forsyth, B., *Andrina*, BBC, 1981

Forsyth, B., *Local Hero: Feature Film and Special Feature: Interview with Writer and Director Bill Forsyth*, Film 4 DVD, 2008

Forsyth, B., *Comfort and Joy*, EMI, 1984

Hudson, H., *Chariots of Fire*, 20th Century Fox, 1981

Kermode, M., 'Interview with Bill Forsyth about *Local Hero*', *The Culture Show*, BBC

Minnelli, V., *Brigadoon*, MGM, 1954

Powell, M. and Pressburger, E., *I Know Where I'm Going*, Rank, 1945

Robertson, J., *Bill Forsyth Lifetime Achievement Film*, Cardonald College

Scott, A., *Getting In on the Action*, NFTS, Beaconsfield, 1983

Whatham, C., *That'll Be the Day*, EMI, 1973

GLOSSARY OF TECHNICAL TERMS

Above the line...................An expenditure that is made before filming begins. A star is 'above the line' because his or her fee must be negotiated separately, whereas other actors will be engaged through casting and paid pro rata.

BAFTA...................................British Academy of Film & Television Arts: this organisation gives annual awards to films and television programmes it considers of outstanding quality. BAFTA Scotland presents its own awards.

Blockbuster.........................A film that achieves widespread popularity and enormous sales, usually as a result of high investment.

Camera angles.................... The angle from which a camera shot is taken, which can affect its meaning e.g. high angle or low angle and the way this can affect the viewer's interpretation of the subject.

Camera shots........................ The distance from which a camera shot is taken, which can affect its meaning e.g. close up or long shot and the way this can affect the viewer's interpretation of the subject.

Camera movements..............The movements a camera can make which can affect a shot's meaning e.g. pan (slow glide from side to side) or tracking shot (where the camera moves along a track) and the way this can affect the viewer's interpretation of the subject.

Casting ....The process used by directors to decide which actors will appear in the film. The decision is made by audition.

Catharsis..............................To cleanse or to purge. In drama it means an emotional cleansing, the witnessing of emotional extremes acting on the audience in a beneficial way.

Corporates............................Short films made for corporations, usually documentaries presenting the achievements of a company or industry in a highly positive way.

Crew..The people behind the camera who plan and physically shoot the film, i.e. locations manager, production manager, camera, sound and lighting.

Distribution ....The means by which a film is moved from its producers to its audience in the cinemas (or, increasingly, on television, DVD or online), often handled by a subsidiary company of the film's backers or by a separate company.

Documentary..........................A film which in some way attempts to 'document' reality.

Diegetic/Non-Diegetic..........Refers to sound in a film. Diegetic music or sound is that which appears within a narrative (e.g. a radio playing), non-diegetic is that which is added to the narrative (e.g. a musical sound track).

Mise-en-scène ....Everything that appears in each shot on the screen, including the positioning of the actors, the angle and distance from which the shot is taken, the costume, acting and props.

Narrative ....In film, this term refers to the entire story within a film, including all the visual and aural methods used to impart meaning to the audience.

Protagonist/Antagonist.......Key characters or elements within a screenplay: the protagonist is usually the central character, or 'hero', the antagonist the character or force who opposes him.

Resolution ....The conclusion to the narrative, often bringing a solution to the challenges encountered by the protagonist during the narrative, either a happy or sad one, but sometimes deliberately left open to audience interpretation (as in the case of the final shot of *Local Hero*).

Rough cut ....The first phase of editing, done during filming, when all scenes and shots which might be used are shown together to allow the director and others to see the progress being made each day. Later editing takes place after the film is completed.

Shapeshifter.........................One of a number of terms to describe character-types used by Christopher Vogler, screenwriting expert and advisor, who derived his ideas from psychoanalysis; a Shapeshifter is a character who changes during the course of a story.

Structure ....Often regarded as the most important element in screenwriting, structure is the story's architecture or shape, organizing it into different phases or sections.

Structuralist ....A critical theory which stresses the importance of a text's structure and content.

Talent ....A term used in the media industries for those who use innate rather than technical or managerial abilities in their work i.e. actors, writers and directors.

Lightning Source UK Ltd.
Milton Keynes UK

172588UK00001B/22/P